D0548466

the stylist's guide to NYC

sibella court

ontents

03

INTRODUCTION

If you're not already super excited about your upcoming NYC adventure, download 'Empire State of Mind' by Jay-Z and Alicia Keys and rock out. PLAY IT LOUD.

This is the most exciting, contained, energy-filled city in the world.

Since moving back to Sydney and opening my shop, The Society Inc, I constantly get asked by customers for my tips and favourite shops, spots and restaurants in NYC. It is so difficult just to choose one as this vibrant, elaborate city has so much to offer (over many trips).

After scouring this amazing city for 15 years I have decided to share some of my loves, secrets and hidden gems. This is my edited, well-tuned style guide to New York.

I have been strict with myself and am sharing my tried and tested places and spaces. I have been frequenting the majority of these places for a very long time and know a lot of the shop owners, managers, shop assistants, public relations people, designers and so on. Feel free to drop my name!

My background is as a stylist, with a love of interiors and all things still-life (well, anything that's beautiful, original and unusual). This is my shopping list. It does not work like a conventional guide and does not include the usual tourist attractions and hotels. However, it is diverse and you may discover things you didn't even know you would enjoy.

I detest backtracking in NYC. This is a habit I picked up while styling there so I have created 'loops of interest' from start to finish. Take your time, pick up where you left off or, if you are fast-paced like me, complete one in a day.

I have invented loose definitions of 'interest' so you can pick and choose. There are nine and some may appeal to you, others may not. They are:

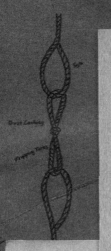

Choco
coa Ni

% cacao

sugar, cocoa

cally with orga
farms in Mada
batches. Hand
ranite stone a

rth: 5/.25,

rothers Chocolat
North 3rd Street
klyn, NY 11211
herschocolate.cc

Vegan product.
used in our facto

can Cr
late

(1) Scents & Flower Merchants

(2) Oddities & Curiosities

(3) Jewellery & Hardware

(4) Haberdashery & Handmade

(5) Drapers & Upholstery

(6) Art & Objets

(7) Paper & Art Supplies

(8) Kitchen & Table Paraphernalia

(9) Furniture & Interiors

For me food is fuel and part of the NYC experience.
Fuel stops are included in my loops as shopping can get
exhausting. Most places are recommended as a package:
food, environment, service and people watching. As you
spend more time in NYC it becomes less of a city and more
of a cluster of distinct villages — with interesting names,
like Tribeca which derives from Triangle Below Canal, SoHo
is South of Houston etc. I'm predominantly a downtown
girl. I lived in Tribeca and Chinatown for 10 years, but
regardless of this, it is my fave place to be.

Every day begins with coffee and snacks for me. So
that's where my loops will start most days. After years of the
worst coffee in the world, NYC has picked up its game and
has a few fabulous baristas around town, thank God!

I encourage you to get distracted, to leave my trail and
follow your fancies. Use the zipcode list at the end of the
book to explore by area. New York is full of discoveries
(I cannot cover everything!!) Look up, scan the information
boards in buildings and see what you are surrounded by.

Take notes on the architecture, manholes, graffiti, shop signage and general street life and personalities. It is all part of the process and there are endless NYC experiences.

These loops are sometimes large and cover a lot of ground, and you may find yourself skipping from one map to the next and back again. Do not feel as if the loops need to be completed in one day. Break them up as you please, pick up where you left off. There is nothing wrong with a long boozy lunch. You're on holidays.

NYC
TIPS

BATHROOMS
When I first moved to NYC I struggled to find bathrooms. Go when you can.

Most restaurants frown upon non-customers and there are very few pubs.

Most of the chain stores, Starbucks, department stores and hotels have bathrooms.

Don't leave it to the last minute.

BE PREPARED FOR ANYTHING
NYC is a city that's about carrying your things and expecting to not necessarily return home.

Day so easily turns into night and you want to be lightweight and prepared for F.U.N.

All good NYC girls carry two pairs of shoes. Take a pair of flats but don't be caught short. Be ready for anything with a killer pair of heels.

It's often quicker to walk the couple of large blocks than take a cab or subway.

A stash of Band-Aids is a must too. Make sure you get the extra wide fabric ones. There's nothing less glamorous than limping around this city or going home early due to blisters!!

The New York weather report is surprisingly correct. If they say it may rain (usually a downpour and short-lived), be sure to take a handbag-size umbrella. However, never fear, if you have left your umbrella at home or do not own one, the street vendors smell rain in the air and are on most corners — you can purchase one for a few dollars.

BICYCLE

I always ride around NYC on a bicycle (except maybe in the dead of winter snowstorms).

The bike lanes are great and are multiplying regularly.

You can rent bikes but not locks.

NYC is notorious for bike theft and it can be devastating. Do not lock your bike to scaffolding. Think about investing in a kryptonite U-lock, they are around US$50 but are well worth the effort (and think what you saved on cabs).

Or you can buy cheap bikes at the flea markets and K-Mart for around US$100.

It's a great way to get to know the city — it's fast, efficient, cheap and makes you smile.

COMMUNICATION

Buy a local pre-paid telephone chip.

T-Mobile has a US$50 month package with phone included!

Purchase in any telephone shop (there are loads on any of the main avenues).

MAPS

Buy a pocket-size pop-up map and a credit card–size subway map.

You can find these at Staples, Barnes & Noble, Kate's Paperie, McNally Jackson.

PARCELS & SHIPPING

When it comes to shipping, most of the larger stores will messenger to your hotel so you don't have to carry your packages. Sometimes they charge a minimal fee (but great value if you are out all day).

Or ask your concierge if they can organise messenger pick-ups before you head out.

Believe me, this is a great service and one not to be dismissed!

For international shipping, I recommend UPS, Fedex or USPS.

SEARCHING

To locate stores, restaurants, museums or even to find out movie times, you can text Google, entering 46645 as the number.

Then enter shop info and name, city or zip. For example, Balthazar NYC or, in the case of movies, *Batman* (or whatever is playing) NYC.

TAXIS & CARS

You cannot call cabs. There are plenty but changeover time is around 3–4pm and can be a pain.

There are a couple of great car services (same price as cabs and negotiable).

Delancey Car Services, (212) 228-3301, and Carmel Car & Limousine Service, (212) 666-3646 in the city. You can dictate what kind of vehicle you need on booking. i.e. mini-van, limo, town car (sedan).

And Northside Car Service, (718) 387-2222 in Brooklyn.

TRANSPORT

Buy a MetroCard at any subway station.

Put $20 on it — it will not go to waste. The subway has large fold-out paper maps (inferior and confusing but ok if you are desperate).

Always take note of which subway exit you take. For example, north east corner of the street or avenue; it can get confusing upon exit but can help you navigate which is north, south, east and west.

New Yorkers are generally a friendly and helpful lot so don't hesitate to ask for directions especially once you get out of the subway. If you are confused, at least ask for compass directions to get you on your way.

WHAT'S ON

Buy *Time Out*, *The New Yorker*, and *New York* magazine for weekly info including museum shows, movies, art shows, sample sales etc. Great to read on the train. I just have to repeat that point: the sample sales are unbelievable in NYC. Most designers have them. Get in early and there are usually big smiles and satisfaction all round.

Great website for local news (esp. Weekend Guides) is DailyCandy. You can subscribe prior to your trip for inspiration.

WHEN TO GO

NYC is a seasonal city so pick your favourite one. I love them all except for high summer (July/August); it's too hot, too humid!

If you are planning to shop and have to adhere to those crazy airline weight restrictions, keep in mind that winter clothes are heavy and take up precious luggage space!

Safe travels &
have a fabulous trip

Enjoy, Sibella X

11

13

PAULA RUBENSTEIN

65 Prince St
NYC 10012

Vintage textiles, furniture and
accessories
Pages 78, 112

JOHN DERIAN COMPANY INC

6 E. 2nd St
NYC 10003
212.677.3917
www.johnderian.com

Textiles, tabletop, accessories and
vintage furniture
Page 81

JOHN ROBSHAW

(by appointment)
245 W. 29th St #1501
NYC 10001
212.594.6006
www.johnrobshaw.com

Furniture and textiles
Page 136

THE END OF HISTORY

548 ½ Hudson St
NYC 10014
212.647.7598
www.theendofhistory.blogspot.com

Mid-century glass
Page 247

LE LABO

233 Elizabeth St
NYC 10012
212.219.2230
www.lelabofragrances.com

Perfumes
Page 40

OCHRE

462 Broome St
NYC 10012
212.414.4332
www.ochre.net

Furniture and accessories
Pages 111, 252

ANTHROPOLOGIE

50 Rockefeller Center
NYC 10020
212.246.0386
www.anthropologie.com

Fashion, beauty, furniture and
homewares
Pages 94, 159, 216

BERGDORF GOODMAN

754 5th Ave
NYC 10019
212.753.7300
www.bergdorfgoodman.com

Homewares, tabletop and fashion
Page 183

PARTNERS & SPADE

40 Great Jones St
NYC 10012
646.861.2827
www.partnersandspade.com

Eclectic objects and art
Page 194

TINSEL TRADING CO

1 W. 37th St
NYC 10018
212.730.1030
www.tinseltrading.com

Haberdashery & notions
Page 129

UNION SQUARE GREENMARKET

Union Square – 14th St and Broadway
(Mon, Wed, Fri, Sat)
NYC 10003

Food market
Page 31

THE RUG COMPANY

88 Wooster St
NYC 10012
212.274.0444
www.therugcompany.info

Rugs
Page 171

CROSBY ST HOTEL

79 Crosby St
NYC 10012
212.226.6400
www.firmdale.com

Hotel
Page 163

SARA

950 Lexington Ave
NYC 10021
212.772.3243
www.saranyc.com

Japanese ceramics and tableware
Page 231

OBSCURA

280 E. 10th St
NYC 10009
212.505.9251
www.obscuraantiques.com

The unlikely and unusual
Page 83

CHELSEA ANTIQUES GARAGE

(Sat & Sun 9-5)
112 W. 25th St
NYC 10001
212.243.5343

Flea market
Pages 55, 225

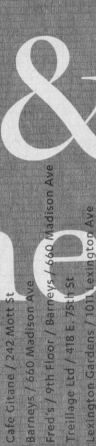

&

me

scents
flower
rchants

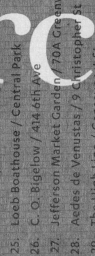

19

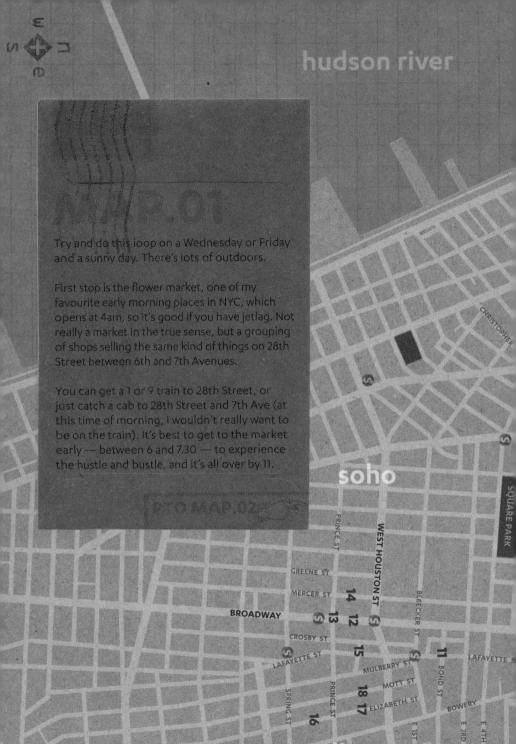

hudson river

M.7 P.01

Try and do this loop on a Wednesday or Friday and a sunny day. There's lots of outdoors.

First stop is the flower market, one of my favourite early morning places in NYC, which opens at 4am, so it's good if you have jetlag. Not really a market in the true sense, but a grouping of shops selling the same kind of things on 28th Street between 6th and 7th Avenues.

You can get a 1 or 9 train to 28th Street, or just catch a cab to 28th Street and 7th Ave (at this time of morning, I wouldn't really want to be on the train). It's best to get to the market early — between 6 and 7.30 — to experience the hustle and bustle, and it's all over by 11.

PTO MAP.02

soho

SQUARE PARK

CHRISTOPHER

PRINCE ST

WEST HOUSTON ST

BLEECKER ST

LAFAYETTE

GREENE ST

MERCER ST

14

12

BROADWAY

13

CROSBY ST

15

11

BOND ST

LAFAYETTE ST

MULBERRY ST

MOTT ST

SPRING ST

PRINCE ST

18 17

ELIZABETH ST

E 1ST ST

BOWERY

E 3RD ST

E 4TH ST

16

nolita

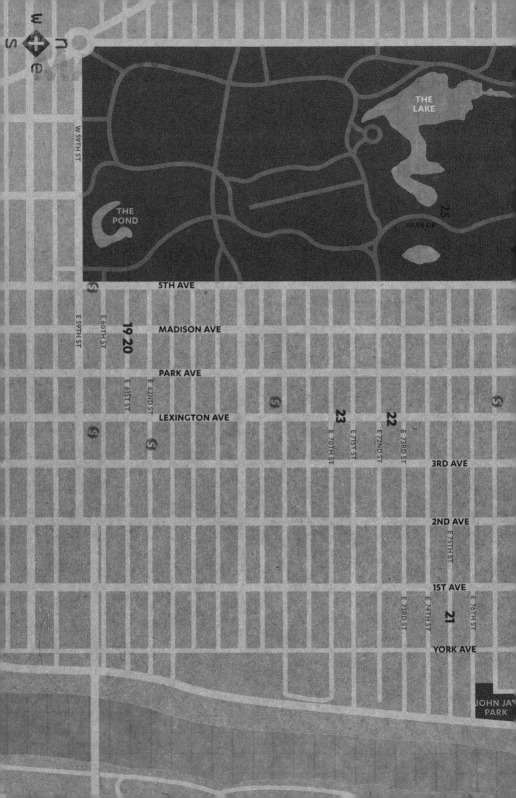

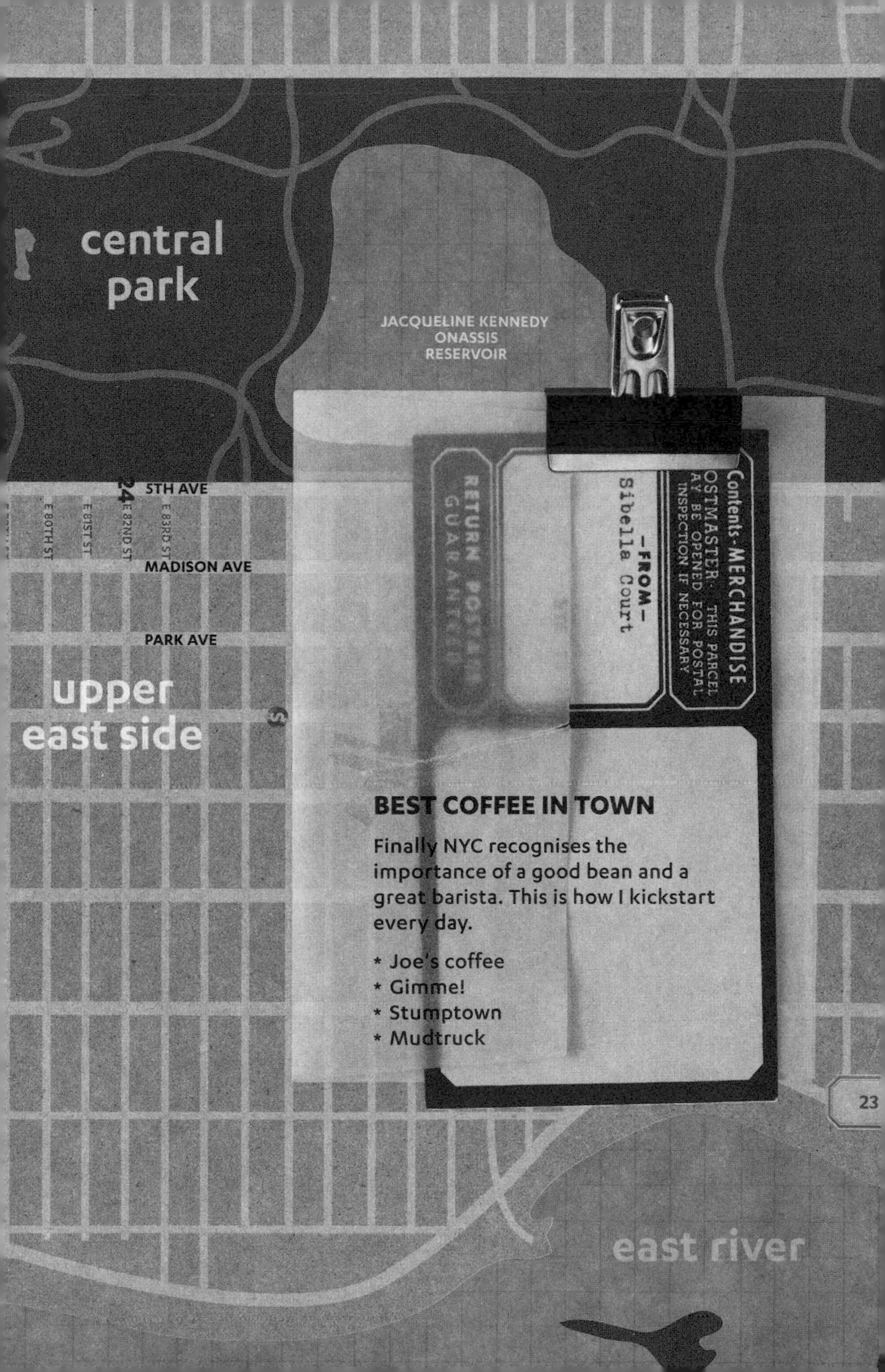

central
park

JACQUELINE KENNEDY
ONASSIS
RESERVOIR

5TH AVE

E 80TH ST
E 81ST ST
E 82ND ST
24
E 83RD ST

MADISON AVE

PARK AVE

upper
east side

RETURN POSTAGE
GUARANTEED

—FROM—
Sibella Court

Contents: MERCHANDISE
OSTMASTER: THIS PARCEL
AY BE OPENED FOR POSTAL
INSPECTION IF NECESSARY

BEST COFFEE IN TOWN

Finally NYC recognises the importance of a good bean and a great barista. This is how I kickstart every day.

* Joe's coffee
* Gimme!
* Stumptown
* Mudtruck

east river

Start at 7th Ave and 28th St, and go to **Planter Resource** (1), a specialty store that sells plant pots, from teeny-weeny to ginormous, in ceramic, plastic, terrazzo, glass and terracotta. They also have a cheap and cheerful glass vase range. Buy in bulk and get it cheaper.

Just as the name suggests, **Designer's Garden** (2) specialises in bonsai and other perfect little sculptures. Check out the hanging snails housing air plants aimed at those with limited space and no garden access. They have miniature succulents that you can buy separately to create your very own miniature desertscape.

The cat's name at **Caribbean Cuts** (3) is Ginger, and he likes attention. Not only do you get all the tropical leaves and flowers but also an unusual selection of sculptural forms: from seeding coconuts, mini pineapples on the stalk, live tumbleweed and lots of other things I don't know the names of. I have bought so so so many things here for photo shoots.

At **G. Page** (4), among the huge selection of imported flowers, look for the seasonal local product unseen elsewhere. I love fiddlehead fern (put it in your hotel room!)

The guys at **28th St Wholesale** (5) are great. They have made hundreds of shoots come together, just by the beauty of the single branch. Magnolia, all kinds of citrus, blossom, dogwood, and even birds' nests in branches. A good selection of cut flowers and air plants as well.

At first sight **B & J Florist Supply** (6) might appear junky. But look closely and you'll find butterflies made of feathers, jars of miniature shells, ropes, string and thread of every variety. All your needs for being crafty can usually be found here. If you're already loaded down, or loaded up, with bits and bobs, you can leave your bags and order a messenger to take them back to where you're staying.

Turn right at 6th Ave and immediately next to McDonalds is **US Evergreens** (7), where you'll find large-scale cut plants and branches from blossom, magnolia, dogwood, willow, mountain laurel, bamboo and every kind of fir imaginable. It's here that you can order fir and magnolia garland by the yard, and wreaths — you know, the kind that are so Christmas in America.

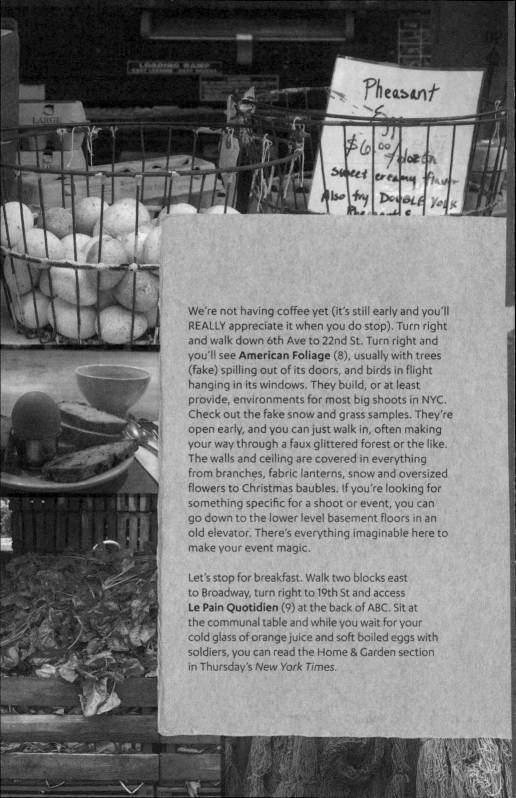

We're not having coffee yet (it's still early and you'll REALLY appreciate it when you do stop). Turn right and walk down 6th Ave to 22nd St. Turn right and you'll see **American Foliage** (8), usually with trees (fake) spilling out of its doors, and birds in flight hanging in its windows. They build, or at least provide, environments for most big shoots in NYC. Check out the fake snow and grass samples. They're open early, and you can just walk in, often making your way through a faux glittered forest or the like. The walls and ceiling are covered in everything from branches, fabric lanterns, snow and oversized flowers to Christmas baubles. If you're looking for something specific for a shoot or event, you can go down to the lower level basement floors in an old elevator. There's everything imaginable here to make your event magic.

Let's stop for breakfast. Walk two blocks east to Broadway, turn right to 19th St and access **Le Pain Quotidien** (9) at the back of ABC. Sit at the communal table and while you wait for your cold glass of orange juice and soft boiled eggs with soldiers, you can read the Home & Garden section in Thursday's *New York Times*.

Walk down Broadway and if it's Monday, Wednesday, Friday or Saturday, the **Union Square Greenmarket** (10) is on. This produce market is strictly seasonal and local. There are so many seasons I love here but in summer when it's strawberry time, you can smell their sweetness from three blocks away! In the fall, winter squash and jack-o'-lantern pumpkins are piled high in their orange and mottled green jackets. And the first of the spring corn can be eaten then and there. It's all good.

My brother Chris craves the Ronnybrook chocolate milk that comes in a glass pint with cream on the top. He rips off the foil top and drinks it straight out of the bottle — straight back to 1975!!!!

Jump in a cab to Bond and Broadway and pop into **Bond No. 9** (11) which has perfumes named after different areas of NYC. I love Riverside Drive even though I want to love Chinatown because the bottle with cherry blossom is so beautiful. Get samples that look like bonbons (wrapped in metallic) — so so so pretty. The bottles are objects to display on their own.

31

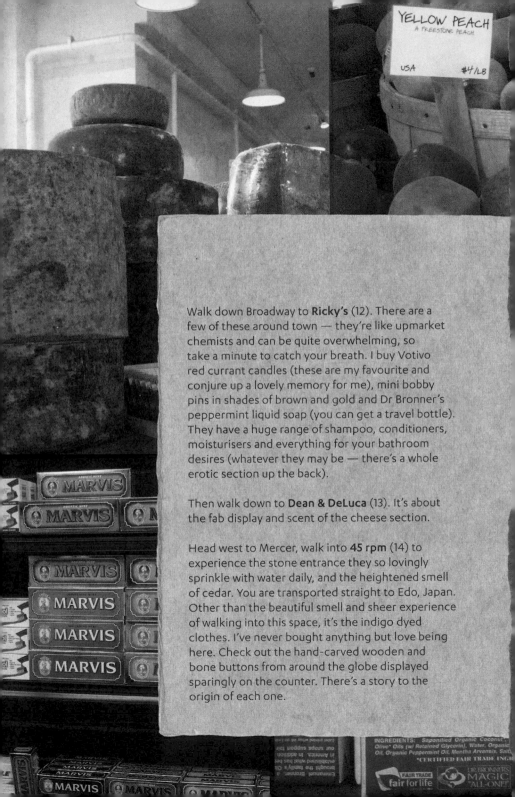

Walk down Broadway to **Ricky's** (12). There are a few of these around town — they're like upmarket chemists and can be quite overwhelming, so take a minute to catch your breath. I buy Votivo red currant candles (these are my favourite and conjure up a lovely memory for me), mini bobby pins in shades of brown and gold and Dr Bronner's peppermint liquid soap (you can get a travel bottle). They have a huge range of shampoo, conditioners, moisturisers and everything for your bathroom desires (whatever they may be — there's a whole erotic section up the back).

Then walk down to **Dean & DeLuca** (13). It's about the fab display and scent of the cheese section.

Head west to Mercer, walk into **45 rpm** (14) to experience the stone entrance they so lovingly sprinkle with water daily, and the heightened smell of cedar. You are transported straight to Edo, Japan. Other than the beautiful smell and sheer experience of walking into this space, it's the indigo dyed clothes. I've never bought anything but love being here. Check out the hand-carved wooden and bone buttons from around the globe displayed sparingly on the counter. There's a story to the origin of each one.

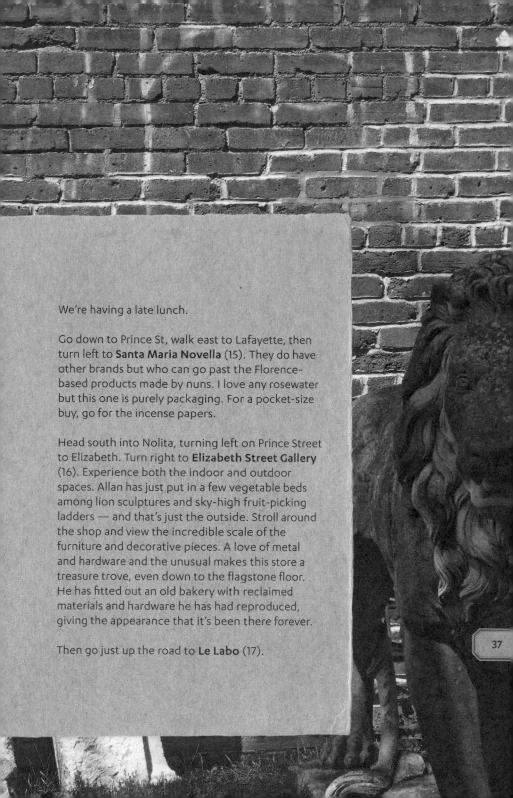

We're having a late lunch.

Go down to Prince St, walk east to Lafayette, then turn left to **Santa Maria Novella** (15). They do have other brands but who can go past the Florence-based products made by nuns. I love any rosewater but this one is purely packaging. For a pocket-size buy, go for the incense papers.

Head south into Nolita, turning left on Prince Street to Elizabeth. Turn right to **Elizabeth Street Gallery** (16). Experience both the indoor and outdoor spaces. Allan has just put in a few vegetable beds among lion sculptures and sky-high fruit-picking ladders — and that's just the outside. Stroll around the shop and view the incredible scale of the furniture and decorative pieces. A love of metal and hardware and the unusual makes this store a treasure trove, even down to the flagstone floor. He has fitted out an old bakery with reclaimed materials and hardware he has had reproduced, giving the appearance that it's been there forever.

Then go just up the road to **Le Labo** (17).

Le Labo

They moved into Shi, one of my favourite shops in New York, after the owner tragically died. It's a beautiful double frontage shop that they have made and branded their own. Industrial in feel, personal in style, a range of perfumes that are packaged for you with your name on them as you wait. I buy rose. Surprise, surprise.

233 Elizabeth St
NYC 10012
212.219.2230
www.lelabofragrances.com

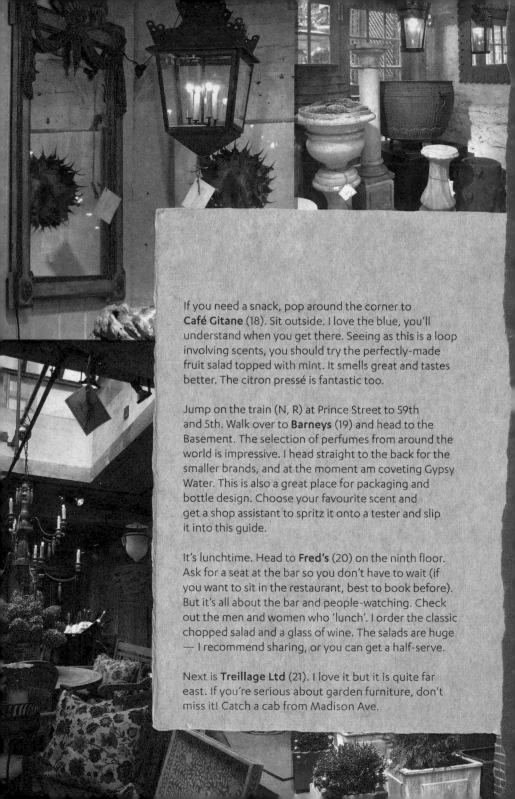

If you need a snack, pop around the corner to **Café Gitane** (18). Sit outside. I love the blue, you'll understand when you get there. Seeing as this is a loop involving scents, you should try the perfectly-made fruit salad topped with mint. It smells great and tastes better. The citron pressé is fantastic too.

Jump on the train (N, R) at Prince Street to 59th and 5th. Walk over to **Barneys** (19) and head to the Basement. The selection of perfumes from around the world is impressive. I head straight to the back for the smaller brands, and at the moment am coveting Gypsy Water. This is also a great place for packaging and bottle design. Choose your favourite scent and get a shop assistant to spritz it onto a tester and slip it into this guide.

It's lunchtime. Head to **Fred's** (20) on the ninth floor. Ask for a seat at the bar so you don't have to wait (if you want to sit in the restaurant, best to book before). But it's all about the bar and people-watching. Check out the men and women who 'lunch'. I order the classic chopped salad and a glass of wine. The salads are huge — I recommend sharing, or you can get a half-serve.

Next is **Treillage Ltd** (21). I love it but it is quite far east. If you're serious about garden furniture, don't miss it! Catch a cab from Madison Ave.

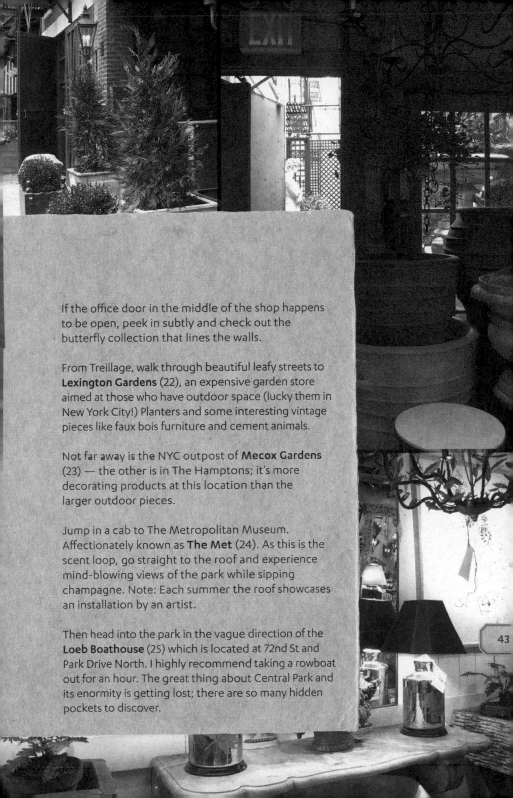

If the office door in the middle of the shop happens to be open, peek in subtly and check out the butterfly collection that lines the walls.

From Treillage, walk through beautiful leafy streets to **Lexington Gardens** (22), an expensive garden store aimed at those who have outdoor space (lucky them in New York City!) Planters and some interesting vintage pieces like faux bois furniture and cement animals.

Not far away is the NYC outpost of **Mecox Gardens** (23) — the other is in The Hamptons; it's more decorating products at this location than the larger outdoor pieces.

Jump in a cab to The Metropolitan Museum. Affectionately known as **The Met** (24). As this is the scent loop, go straight to the roof and experience mind-blowing views of the park while sipping champagne. Note: Each summer the roof showcases an installation by an artist.

Then head into the park in the vague direction of the **Loeb Boathouse** (25) which is located at 72nd St and Park Drive North. I highly recommend taking a rowboat out for an hour. The great thing about Central Park and its enormity is getting lost; there are so many hidden pockets to discover.

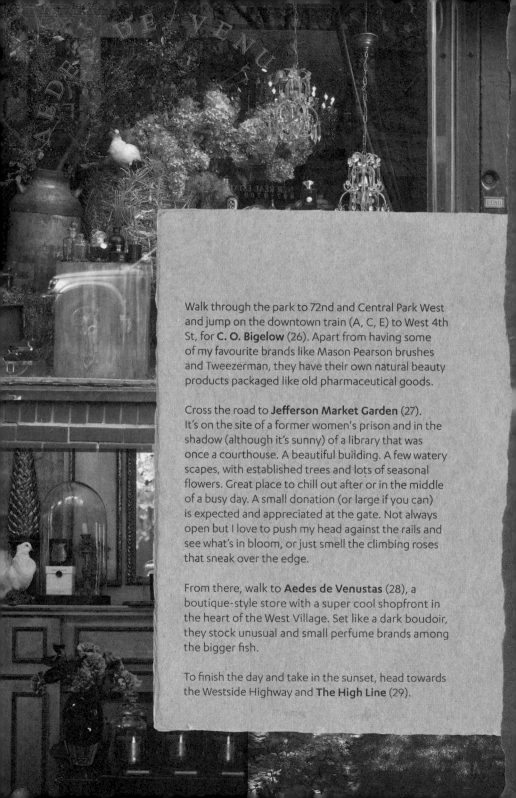

Walk through the park to 72nd and Central Park West and jump on the downtown train (A, C, E) to West 4th St, for **C. O. Bigelow** (26). Apart from having some of my favourite brands like Mason Pearson brushes and Tweezerman, they have their own natural beauty products packaged like old pharmaceutical goods.

Cross the road to **Jefferson Market Garden** (27). It's on the site of a former women's prison and in the shadow (although it's sunny) of a library that was once a courthouse. A beautiful building. A few watery scapes, with established trees and lots of seasonal flowers. Great place to chill out after or in the middle of a busy day. A small donation (or large if you can) is expected and appreciated at the gate. Not always open but I love to push my head against the rails and see what's in bloom, or just smell the climbing roses that sneak over the edge.

From there, walk to **Aedes de Venustas** (28), a boutique-style store with a super cool shopfront in the heart of the West Village. Set like a dark boudoir, they stock unusual and small perfume brands among the bigger fish.

To finish the day and take in the sunset, head towards the Westside Highway and **The High Line** (29).

The High Line

The elevated garden starts at Gansevoort Street but can be accessed at various points into the 30s along Washington St and 10th Ave. This is a beautiful way to complete the loop. This old, disused railway track which delivered products to warehouses was converted, and continues to be converted, into a beautiful oasis. It's just divine. There are big, wooden sunbeds where you can enjoy a cheeky glass of wine (with the wine you picked up on the way from any liquor store); rambling, seasonal gardens (there's always something flowering); voyeurism opportunities through people's loft windows; viewing stations and Hudson River views.

529 W. 20th St #8W
NYC 10011
212.206.9922
www.thehighline.org

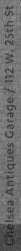

odd
cur

lities &
iosities

49

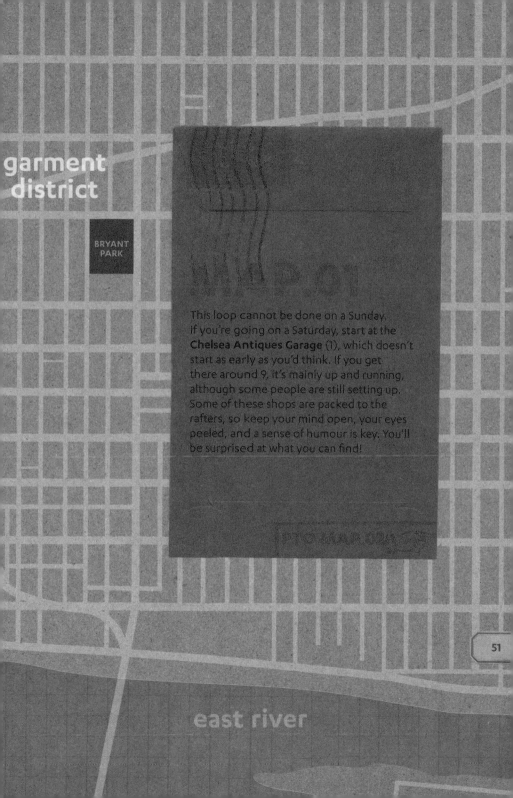

garment
district

BRYANT
PARK

This loop cannot be done on a Sunday.
If you're going on a Saturday, start at the
Chelsea Antiques Garage (1), which doesn't
start as early as you'd think. If you get
there around 9, it's mainly up and running,
although some people are still setting up.
Some of these shops are packed to the
rafters, so keep your mind open, your eyes
peeled, and a sense of humour is key. You'll
be surprised at what you can find!

PTO MAP.02

east river

n
w e
s

7TH AVE

CARMINE ST
14
DOWNING ST
15

west village

SPRING ST

VARICK ST

soho

6TH AVE

MACDOUGAL ST

SULLIVAN ST

17

5TH AVE

CANAL ST

13

12

THOMPSON ST

16

WASHINGTON SQUARE PARK

WEST BROADWAY

BROOME ST

SPRING ST

PRINCE ST

WEST HOUSTON ST

BLEECKER ST

W 3RD ST

WOOSTER ST

21

20

GREENE ST

18

19

CANAL ST

HOWARD ST

GRAND ST

MERCER ST

22

BROADWAY

CROSBY ST

27

BROADWAY

23

24

25

26

LAFAYETTE ST

LAFAYETTE ST

E 2ND ST

little italy

MULBERRY ST

PRINCE ST

MOTT ST

35

BOWERY

3RD AVE

E 5TH ST

E 7TH ST

E 8TH ST

E 9TH ST

31 32

2ND AVE

east village

HESTER ST

GRAND ST

ELIZABETH ST

BOWERY

28

E 1ST ST

E 3RD ST

nolita

29

30

CHRYSTIE ST

SARA D ROOSEVELT PARK

DELANCEY ST

RIVINGTON ST

EAST HOUSTON ST

1ST AVE

E 2ND ST

E 4TH ST

E 6TH ST

33

AVENUE A

TOMPKINS SQUARE PARK

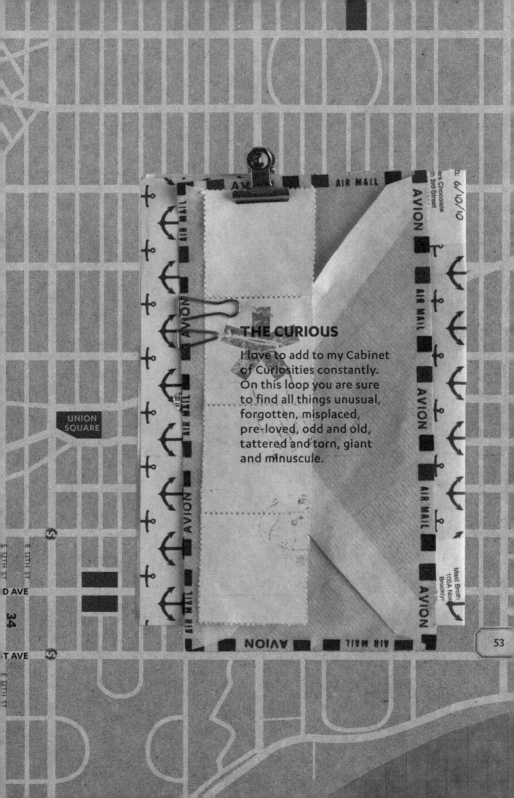

THE CURIOUS

I love to add to my Cabinet of Curiosities constantly. On this loop you are sure to find all things unusual, forgotten, misplaced, pre-loved, odd and old, tattered and torn, giant and minuscule.

Chelsea Antiques Garage

I love both floors and find lots of goodies.
Some of my favourite discoveries were a giant
weather-beaten antler, tiny glass bottles of
labelled pigment, a cast-iron string holder
and vintage luggage labels. There are a couple
of standout stalls; however, it is constantly
changing, so just peruse. You'll find fantastic
vintage furniture, letters and postcards, badges,
botanical and scientific etchings, quilts and linen,
and other treasures from past eras. Among all
this are jam-packed African and Chinese stalls:
porcelain figurines, trade beads, mud cloth,
wooden and beaded stools, jade and coral.

(Sat & Sun 9-5)
112 W. 25th St
NYC 10001
212.243.5343

From there, walk to the **outdoor market** (2) on West 25th between 5th and 6th — it's the last one left in the area. There used to be lots and lots but they're now buildings.

After you've foraged through the markets, walk over to Broadway and stop for a coffee and snack in the **Ace Hotel foyer** (3). If it's not the weekend, you can start your loop here. Order coffee and a croissant from **Stumptown Coffee Roasters** as you sit in the detail-oriented interior by Roman and Williams. Check out the fresh flowers, the use of different materials from tartan to leather and even the pianola scrolls that wallpaper the ground floor bathrooms. A new way of interpreting the function of the lobby — everything happens here.

Note: If you're here after 10, go to **Opening Ceremony**. They have a cool selection of random bits and bobs including collaborations with the likes of Moleskine. I bought pharmaceuticals called 'help: I have a blister' where it was all about the packaging.

From here, walk one block to 28th St and then west to **Jamali Floral & Garden Supplies** (4).

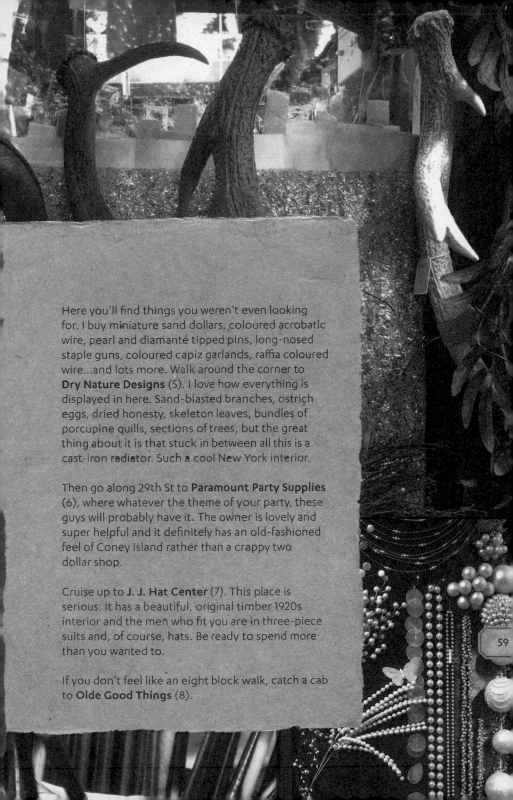

Here you'll find things you weren't even looking for. I buy miniature sand dollars, coloured acrobatic wire, pearl and diamanté tipped pins, long-nosed staple guns, coloured capiz garlands, raffia coloured wire...and lots more. Walk around the corner to **Dry Nature Designs** (5). I love how everything is displayed in here. Sand-blasted branches, ostrich eggs, dried honesty, skeleton leaves, bundles of porcupine quills, sections of trees, but the great thing about it is that stuck in between all this is a cast-iron radiator. Such a cool New York interior.

Then go along 29th St to **Paramount Party Supplies** (6), where whatever the theme of your party, these guys will probably have it. The owner is lovely and super helpful and it definitely has an old-fashioned feel of Coney Island rather than a crappy two dollar shop.

Cruise up to **J. J. Hat Center** (7). This place is serious. It has a beautiful, original timber 1920s interior and the men who fit you are in three-piece suits and, of course, hats. Be ready to spend more than you wanted to.

If you don't feel like an eight block walk, catch a cab to **Olde Good Things** (8).

Olde Good Things

This is a great resource for salvaged pieces. They have a huge warehouse somewhere out of New York, so if you're looking for a specific piece, don't be shy to ask as they are more than willing to bring things in for you. On a larger scale, their range of doors, shutters, bathtubs, tables and sinks is exciting — the doors you find might be from The Plaza! A huge selection of cabinetry hardware, bathroom fixtures, tapware, shower roses, luggage racks, coat hooks, shelf brackets. Beautiful, all-American.

124 W. 24th St
NYC 10011
212.989.8401
www.ogtstore.com

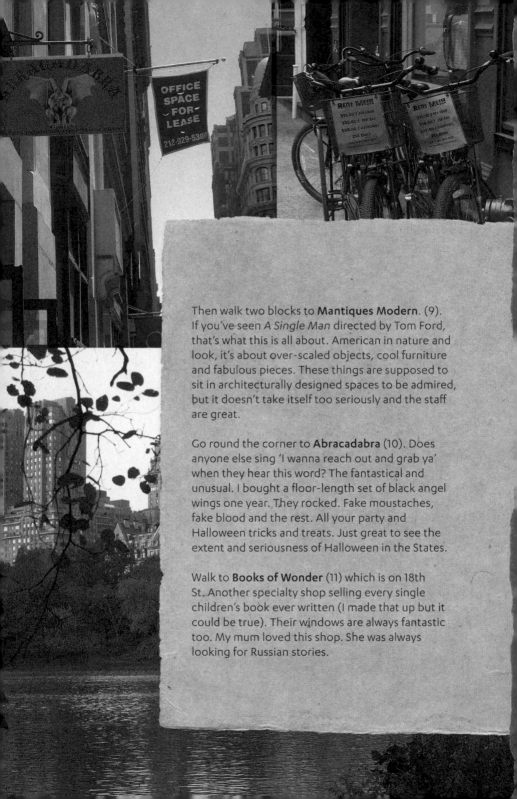

Then walk two blocks to **Mantiques Modern**. (9). If you've seen *A Single Man* directed by Tom Ford, that's what this is all about. American in nature and look, it's about over-scaled objects, cool furniture and fabulous pieces. These things are supposed to sit in architecturally designed spaces to be admired, but it doesn't take itself too seriously and the staff are great.

Go round the corner to **Abracadabra** (10). Does anyone else sing 'I wanna reach out and grab ya' when they hear this word? The fantastical and unusual. I bought a floor-length set of black angel wings one year. They rocked. Fake moustaches, fake blood and the rest. All your party and Halloween tricks and treats. Just great to see the extent and seriousness of Halloween in the States.

Walk to **Books of Wonder** (11) which is on 18th St. Another specialty shop selling every single children's book ever written (I made that up but it could be true). Their windows are always fantastic too. My mum loved this shop. She was always looking for Russian stories.

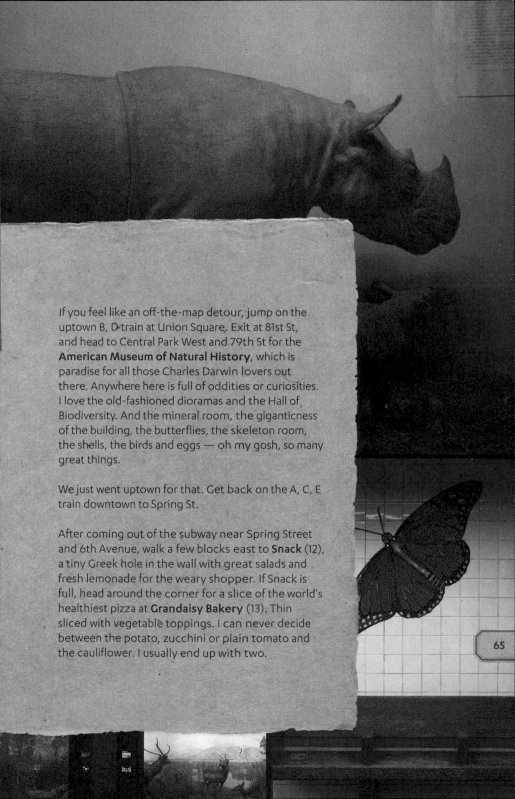

If you feel like an off-the-map detour, jump on the uptown B, D train at Union Square. Exit at 81st St, and head to Central Park West and 79th St for the **American Museum of Natural History**, which is paradise for all those Charles Darwin lovers out there. Anywhere here is full of oddities or curiosities. I love the old-fashioned dioramas and the Hall of Biodiversity. And the mineral room, the giganticness of the building, the butterflies, the skeleton room, the shells, the birds and eggs — oh my gosh, so many great things.

We just went uptown for that. Get back on the A, C, E train downtown to Spring St.

After coming out of the subway near Spring Street and 6th Avenue, walk a few blocks east to **Snack** (12), a tiny Greek hole in the wall with great salads and fresh lemonade for the weary shopper. If Snack is full, head around the corner for a slice of the world's healthiest pizza at **Grandaisy Bakery** (13). Thin sliced with vegetable toppings. I can never decide between the potato, zucchini or plain tomato and the cauliflower. I usually end up with two.

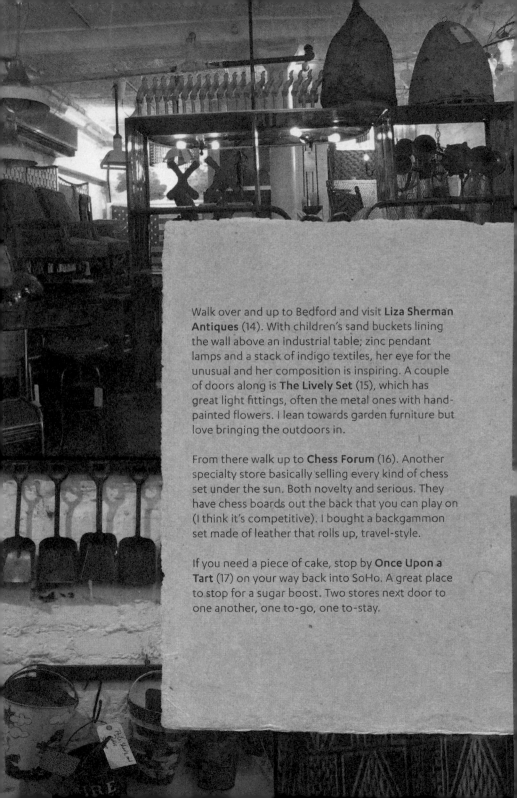

Walk over and up to Bedford and visit **Liza Sherman Antiques** (14). With children's sand buckets lining the wall above an industrial table; zinc pendant lamps and a stack of indigo textiles, her eye for the unusual and her composition is inspiring. A couple of doors along is **The Lively Set** (15), which has great light fittings, often the metal ones with hand-painted flowers. I lean towards garden furniture but love bringing the outdoors in.

From there walk up to **Chess Forum** (16). Another specialty store basically selling every kind of chess set under the sun. Both novelty and serious. They have chess boards out the back that you can play on (I think it's competitive). I bought a backgammon set made of leather that rolls up, travel-style.

If you need a piece of cake, stop by **Once Upon a Tart** (17) on your way back into SoHo. A great place to stop for a sugar boost. Two stores next door to one another, one to-go, one to-stay.

GIANT CLAMS
OTHER SIZES
AVAILABLE

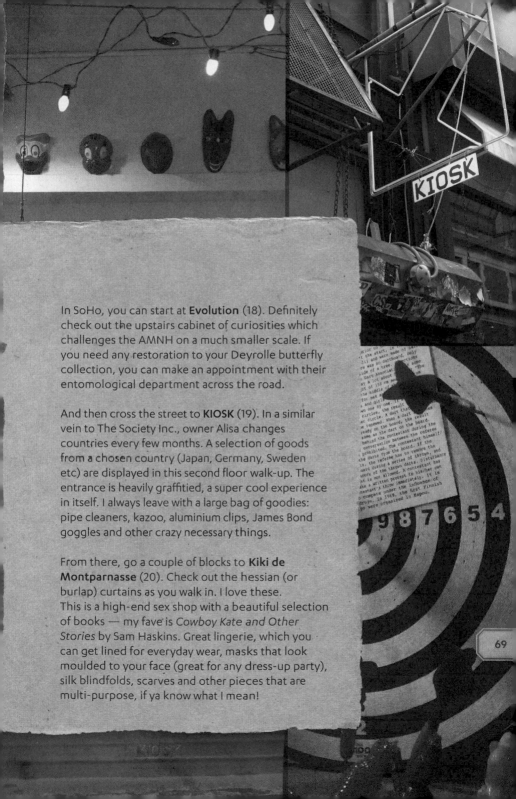

In SoHo, you can start at **Evolution** (18). Definitely check out the upstairs cabinet of curiosities which challenges the AMNH on a much smaller scale. If you need any restoration to your Deyrolle butterfly collection, you can make an appointment with their entomological department across the road.

And then cross the street to **KIOSK** (19). In a similar vein to The Society Inc., owner Alisa changes countries every few months. A selection of goods from a chosen country (Japan, Germany, Sweden etc) are displayed in this second floor walk-up. The entrance is heavily graffitied, a super cool experience in itself. I always leave with a large bag of goodies: pipe cleaners, kazoo, aluminium clips, James Bond goggles and other crazy necessary things.

From there, go a couple of blocks to **Kiki de Montparnasse** (20). Check out the hessian (or burlap) curtains as you walk in. I love these. This is a high-end sex shop with a beautiful selection of books — my fave is *Cowboy Kate and Other Stories* by Sam Haskins. Great lingerie, which you can get lined for everyday wear, masks that look moulded to your face (great for any dress-up party), silk blindfolds, scarves and other pieces that are multi-purpose, if ya know what I mean!

Down the block is **Jack Spade** (21), a quirky, curious store selling mainly canvas messenger bags, wet-packs, overnight bags and wallets for men. Among these utilitarian-style things are odd bits and pieces that I always love: rubber bands that split into four, knot-tying instructions and doctors' paddlepop sticks that read 'I was born on a pirate ship'.

Walk two blocks east to **Pearl River** (22). I used to go to this Chinese department store when it was located on the corner of Broadway and Canal. It was an upstairs gig, and probably a fire hazard, but I loved the higgledy-piggledy-ness of it all. It's not like that anymore — but still a great variety of both rubbish and quality products. An interesting porcelain and ceramic section, paper garlands, the cotton Chinese pyjamas I used to wear as a kid, tin wind-up toys and paper lanterns galore.

Walk over to Crosby Street, and then head south to **De Vera** (23).

De Vera

Originally a San Franciscan shop, now in a classic downtown wrought-iron corner building. Beautiful and sunny, you are met at the door by a brass vessel of growing moss. This is only the start. Sometimes more museum than shop, it houses the curious, the unusual, the handmade, in a well thought-out display space. Take your time and really look; you'll come across anything from Chinese kingfisher hairpins to bone combs to knot-rings, moonstone eggs, cast hands and everything in between.

1 Crosby St
NYC 10013
212.625.0838
www.deveraobjects.com

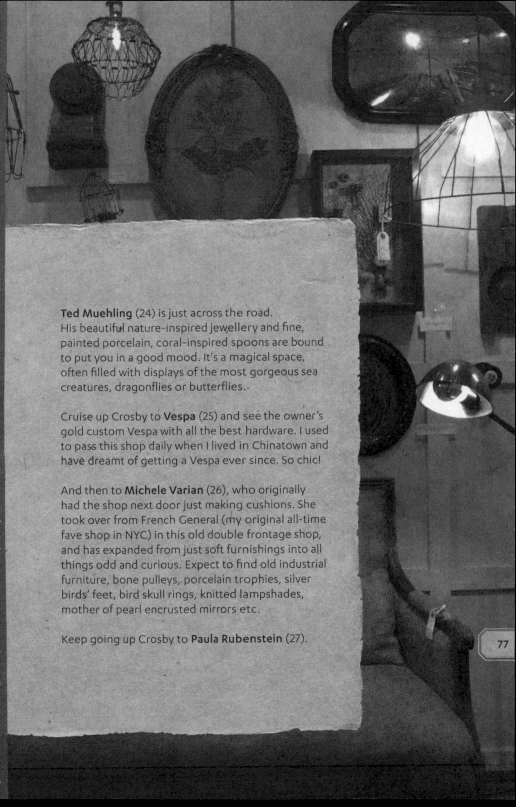

Ted Muehling (24) is just across the road. His beautiful nature-inspired jewellery and fine, painted porcelain, coral-inspired spoons are bound to put you in a good mood. It's a magical space, often filled with displays of the most gorgeous sea creatures, dragonflies or butterflies.

Cruise up Crosby to **Vespa** (25) and see the owner's gold custom Vespa with all the best hardware. I used to pass this shop daily when I lived in Chinatown and have dreamt of getting a Vespa ever since. So chic!

And then to **Michele Varian** (26), who originally had the shop next door just making cushions. She took over from French General (my original all-time fave shop in NYC) in this old double frontage shop, and has expanded from just soft furnishings into all things odd and curious. Expect to find old industrial furniture, bone pulleys, porcelain trophies, silver birds' feet, bird skull rings, knitted lampshades, mother of pearl encrusted mirrors etc.

Keep going up Crosby to **Paula Rubenstein** (27).

Paula Rubenstein

OK, this REALLY is my all-time favourite store in New York. Paula is a fixture at all the local flea markets in the area — she's savvy, with a sophisticated and knowledgeable eye. Her store is an extension of herself — expect to find ticking, American-Indian rugs, natural dyed linen, chintz, floral print, indigo, ribbons, mannequins, metal letters, giant string balls, knot tied balls, things found in artists studios, ship chain, photographs of sailing boats, leather balls (both medicinal and sport), books, blocks, braids, bolts...I hope you're getting the gist. Expect the unexpected, and always vintage.

65 Prince St
NYC 10012
212.966.8954

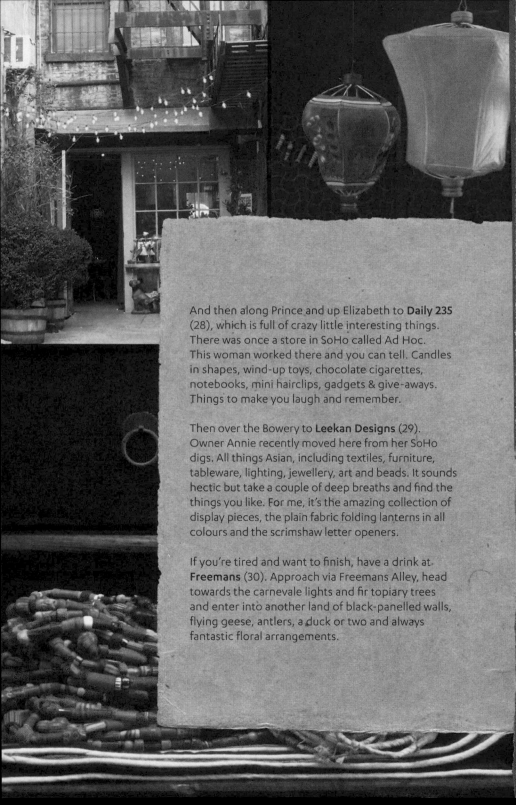

And then along Prince and up Elizabeth to **Daily 235** (28), which is full of crazy little interesting things. There was once a store in SoHo called Ad Hoc. This woman worked there and you can tell. Candles in shapes, wind-up toys, chocolate cigarettes, notebooks, mini hairclips, gadgets & give-aways. Things to make you laugh and remember.

Then over the Bowery to **Leekan Designs** (29). Owner Annie recently moved here from her SoHo digs. All things Asian, including textiles, furniture, tableware, lighting, jewellery, art and beads. It sounds hectic but take a couple of deep breaths and find the things you like. For me, it's the amazing collection of display pieces, the plain fabric folding lanterns in all colours and the scrimshaw letter openers.

If you're tired and want to finish, have a drink at **Freemans** (30). Approach via Freemans Alley, head towards the carnevale lights and fir topiary trees and enter into another land of black-panelled walls, flying geese, antlers, a duck or two and always fantastic floral arrangements.

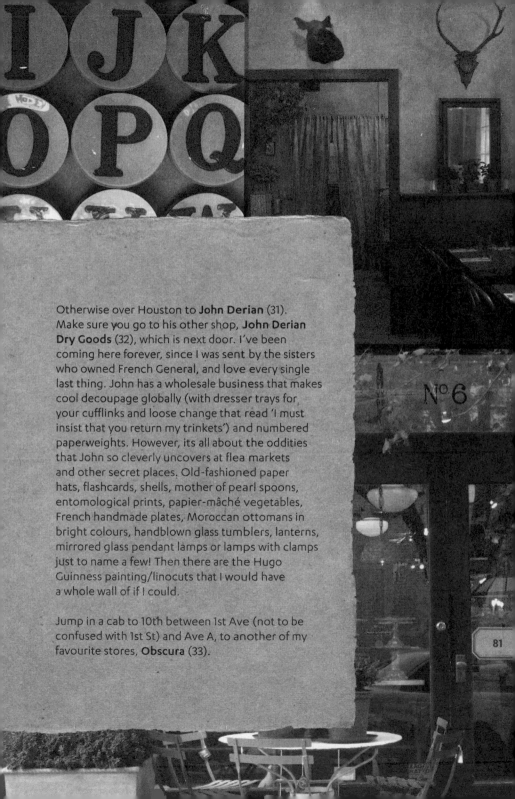

Otherwise over Houston to **John Derian** (31).
Make sure you go to his other shop, **John Derian
Dry Goods** (32), which is next door. I've been
coming here forever, since I was sent by the sisters
who owned French General, and love every single
last thing. John has a wholesale business that makes
cool decoupage globally (with dresser trays for
your cufflinks and loose change that read 'I must
insist that you return my trinkets') and numbered
paperweights. However, its all about the oddities
that John so cleverly uncovers at flea markets
and other secret places. Old-fashioned paper
hats, flashcards, shells, mother of pearl spoons,
entomological prints, papier-mâché vegetables,
French handmade plates, Moroccan ottomans in
bright colours, handblown glass tumblers, lanterns,
mirrored glass pendant lamps or lamps with clamps
just to name a few! Then there are the Hugo
Guinness painting/linocuts that I would have
a whole wall of if I could.

Jump in a cab to 10th between 1st Ave (not to be
confused with 1st St) and Ave A, to another of my
favourite stores, **Obscura** (33).

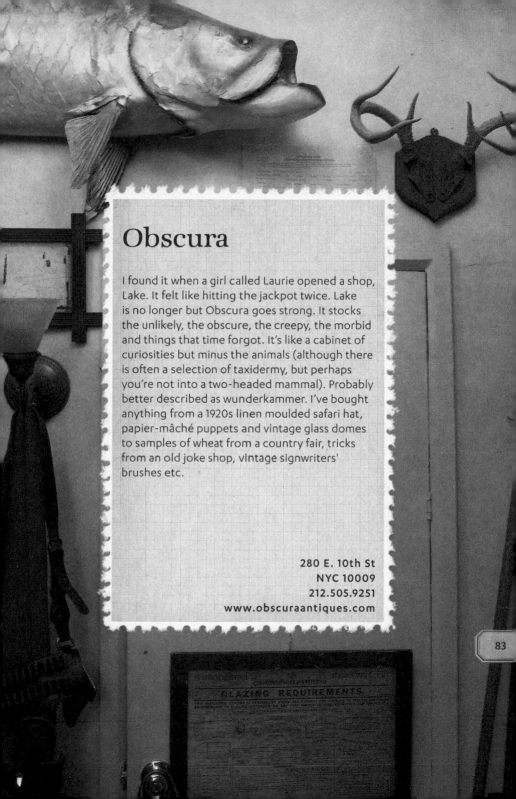

Obscura

I found it when a girl called Laurie opened a shop, Lake. It felt like hitting the jackpot twice. Lake is no longer but Obscura goes strong. It stocks the unlikely, the obscure, the creepy, the morbid and things that time forgot. It's like a cabinet of curiosities but minus the animals (although there is often a selection of taxidermy, but perhaps you're not into a two-headed mammal). Probably better described as wunderkammer. I've bought anything from a 1920s linen moulded safari hat, papier-mâché puppets and vintage glass domes to samples of wheat from a country fair, tricks from an old joke shop, vintage signwriters' brushes etc.

280 E. 10th St
NYC 10009
212.505.9251
www.obscuraantiques.com

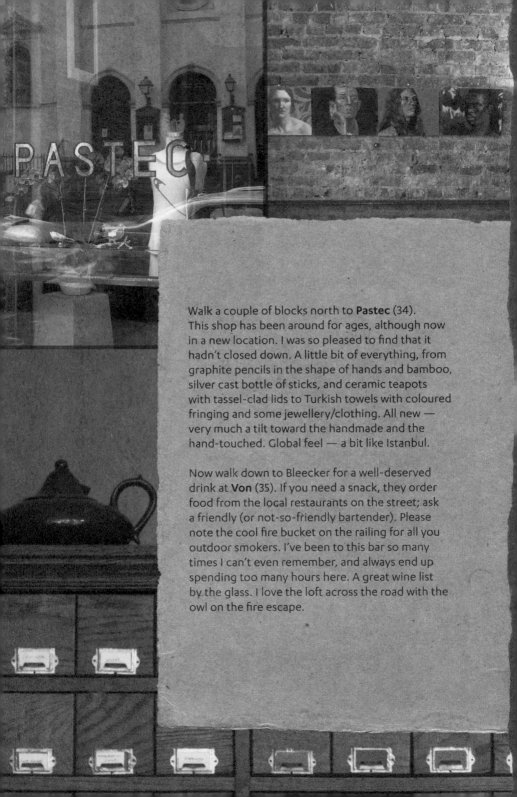

Walk a couple of blocks north to **Pastec** (34).
This shop has been around for ages, although now
in a new location. I was so pleased to find that it
hadn't closed down. A little bit of everything, from
graphite pencils in the shape of hands and bamboo,
silver cast bottle of sticks, and ceramic teapots
with tassel-clad lids to Turkish towels with coloured
fringing and some jewellery/clothing. All new —
very much a tilt toward the handmade and the
hand-touched. Global feel — a bit like Istanbul.

Now walk down to Bleecker for a well-deserved
drink at **Von** (35). If you need a snack, they order
food from the local restaurants on the street; ask
a friendly (or not-so-friendly bartender). Please
note the cool fire bucket on the railing for all you
outdoor smokers. I've been to this bar so many
times I can't even remember, and always end up
spending too many hours here. A great wine list
by the glass. I love the loft across the road with the
owl on the fire escape.

jewe
ha

888 Broadway

llery &
rdware

89

hudson river

chelsea

N E S W

8TH AVE

W 18TH ST
W 19TH ST
W 20TH ST
W 21ST ST

7TH AVE

W 14TH ST

W 23RD ST

5

6TH AVE

6 **7**

W 18TH ST
W 19TH ST

4

5TH AVE

5TH AVE

E 14TH ST

8

BROADWAY

9

MADISON
SQUARE
PARK

E 20TH ST
E 21ST ST
E 23RD ST

MADISON AVE

UNION
SQUARE

PARK AVE SOUTH

gramercy

LEXINGTON AVE

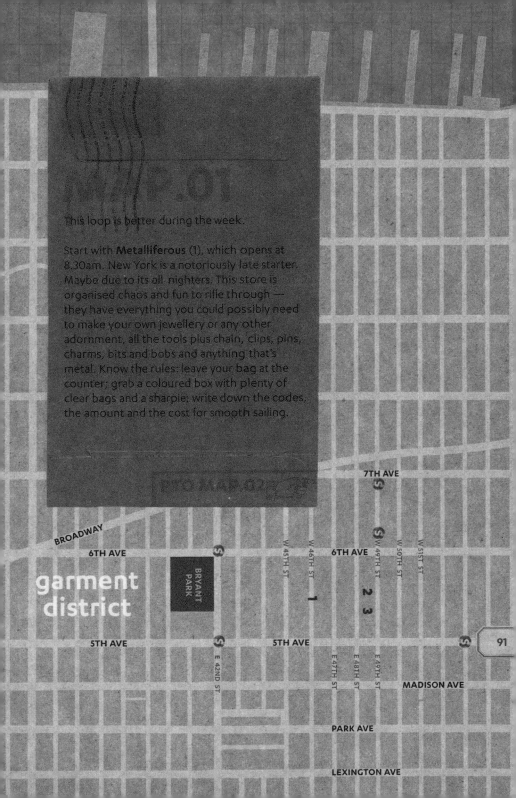

MAP P.01

This loop is better during the week.

Start with **Metalliferous** (1), which opens at 8.30am. New York is a notoriously late starter. Maybe due to its all-nighters. This store is organised chaos and fun to rifle through — they have everything you could possibly need to make your own jewellery or any other adornment, all the tools plus chain, clips, pins, charms, bits and bobs and anything that's metal. Know the rules: leave your bag at the counter; grab a coloured box with plenty of clear bags and a sharpie; write down the codes, the amount and the cost for smooth sailing.

PTO MAP.02

BROADWAY

6TH AVE

garment district

BRYANT PARK

W 45TH ST
W 46TH ST

7TH AVE

6TH AVE

W 49TH ST
W 50TH ST
W 51ST ST

1

2
3

5TH AVE

5TH AVE

E 42ND ST

E 47TH ST
E 48TH ST
E 49TH ST

MADISON AVE

PARK AVE

LEXINGTON AVE

MAP 02

CHAMBERS ST

BROADWAY

TO BUILD A SET

The places that sell and rent
all you need to build and
photograph your set for the
latest magazine or advertising
campaign you're working on.

* The Set Shop
* Prince Lumber
* AKA Locations
* Milk Studios
* Jamali

east river

hudson river

WEST ST

N MOORE ST

GREENWICH ST

CANAL ST

HUDSON ST

FRANKLIN ST

11 VESTRY ST

VARICK ST

soho

6TH AVE

HUDSON ST

10

12 tribeca

WASHINGTON SQUARE PARK

LEONARD ST

WHITE ST

W BROADWAY

BROOME ST

SPRING ST

WEST HOUSTON ST

BLEECKER ST

13

WOOSTER ST

CHURCH ST

GREENE ST

14 15

FRANKLIN ST

CANAL ST

GRAND ST

MERCER ST

21

PRINCE ST

E 2ND ST

16

17 HOWARD ST

18 19

20

BROADWAY

CROSBY ST

LAFAYETTE ST

22 23 24 25

26

BOWERY

E 3RD ST

LAFAYETTE ST

MULBERRY ST

MOTT ST

little
italy

nolita

E 1ST ST

ELIZABETH ST

GRAND ST

HESTER ST

BOWERY

27

CHRYSTIE ST

east
village

SARA D ROOSEVELT PARK

DELANCEY ST

RIVINGTON ST

EAST HOUSTON ST

93

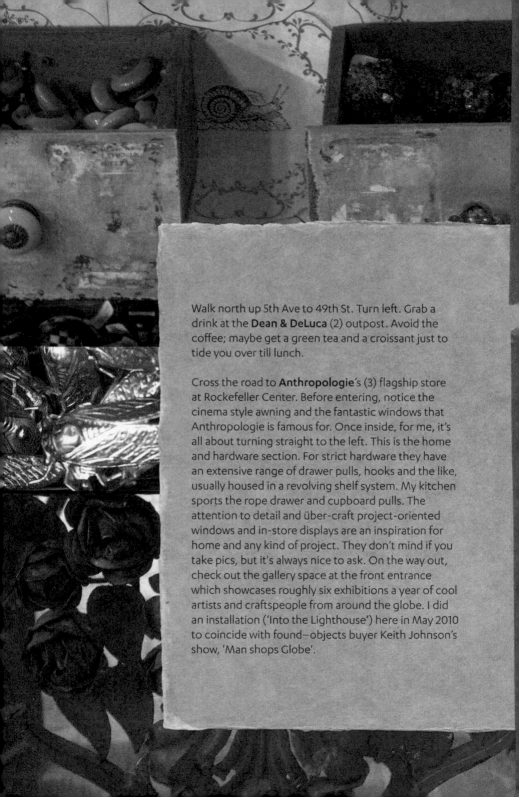

Walk north up 5th Ave to 49th St. Turn left. Grab a
drink at the **Dean & DeLuca** (2) outpost. Avoid the
coffee; maybe get a green tea and a croissant just to
tide you over till lunch.

Cross the road to **Anthropologie**'s (3) flagship store
at Rockefeller Center. Before entering, notice the
cinema style awning and the fantastic windows that
Anthropologie is famous for. Once inside, for me, it's
all about turning straight to the left. This is the home
and hardware section. For strict hardware they have
an extensive range of drawer pulls, hooks and the like,
usually housed in a revolving shelf system. My kitchen
sports the rope drawer and cupboard pulls. The
attention to detail and über-craft project-oriented
windows and in-store displays are an inspiration for
home and any kind of project. They don't mind if you
take pics, but it's always nice to ask. On the way out,
check out the gallery space at the front entrance
which showcases roughly six exhibitions a year of cool
artists and craftspeople from around the globe. I did
an installation ('Into the Lighthouse') here in May 2010
to coincide with found—objects buyer Keith Johnson's
show, 'Man shops Globe'.

Let's catch the train from 50th and 7th Ave station (1, 2, 3) downtown to 14th St for **Lighting & Beyond** (4). After I split with my electrician boyfriend (he worked on films) I taught myself basic electrical skills. I love buying all the components to make my own pendants. Here you can get the plug, the cloth-covered cord, the dimmer, the lightbulb bracket, the shade and even the on-off pull. And all these come in a variety of options. Make it yourself, make it personal, and watch out for shocks. Keep in mind the cord works anywhere in the world as long as you change the lightbulb.

Walk up 6th Ave to 18th St, turn left and go into **West Elm** (5), which is cheap and cheerful without much integrity. But I do buy their curtain rail holders that I convert and use to make rope banisters.

Head east to 6th Ave, and **Bed Bath & Beyond** (6). It's huge and it's ugly and it's pedestrian — but it's got all the basics. Go straight to the coat-hanger section (the caramel velvety ones are great for dresses and come in children sized) and ballbearing shower curtain hooks.

Go across the road to **The Container Store** (7). I'm not a huge fan of the chain but this place has a great selection of unusual shaped shopping bags, boxes, hooks, large elastic bands and other random bits and pieces.

Walk toward 5th to **Waterworks** (8). I remember the first time I walked in here and got excited about bathroom fittings. Great vignettes in store and they ship globally. Tile selection, shower roses and tap fixtures with a selection of accessories.

Then it's over to **Canopy Designs** (9) at ABC Carpet & Home. Quirky unusual chandelier and wall sconces. I feel like I'm Marie Antoinette when I'm among all these amazing lights. I love the beaded ship chandelier. Take your time to look at the great selection of jewellery here as well.

It's lunchtime.

Jump in a cab and head to **Smith & Mills** (10).

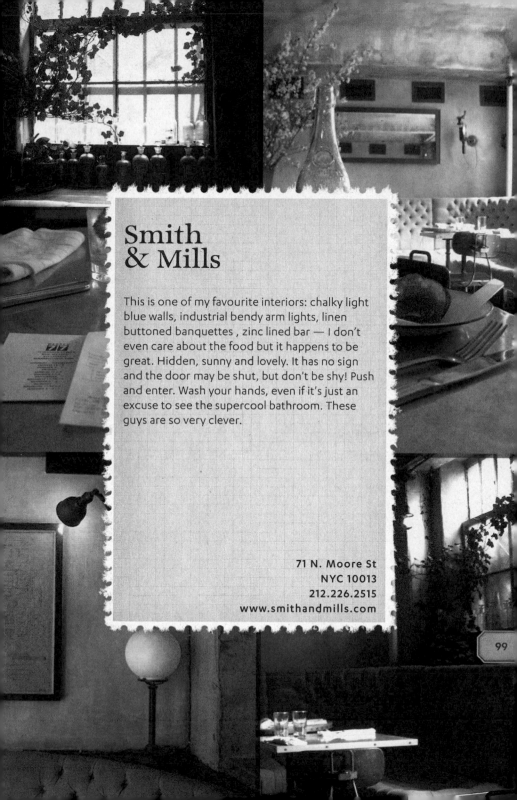

Smith
& Mills

This is one of my favourite interiors: chalky light blue walls, industrial bendy arm lights, linen buttoned banquettes , zinc lined bar — I don't even care about the food but it happens to be great. Hidden, sunny and lovely. It has no sign and the door may be shut, but don't be shy! Push and enter. Wash your hands, even if it's just an excuse to see the supercool bathroom. These guys are so very clever.

71 N. Moore St
NYC 10013
212.226.2515
www.smithandmills.com

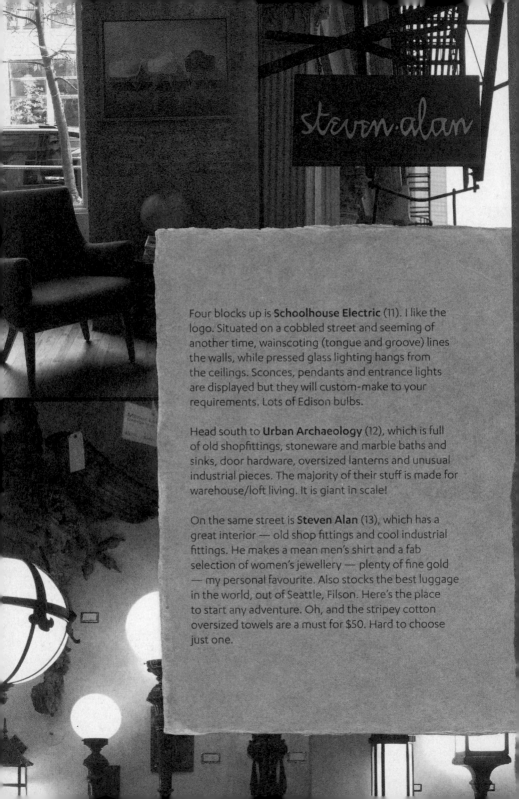

Four blocks up is **Schoolhouse Electric** (11). I like the logo. Situated on a cobbled street and seeming of another time, wainscoting (tongue and groove) lines the walls, while pressed glass lighting hangs from the ceilings. Sconces, pendants and entrance lights are displayed but they will custom-make to your requirements. Lots of Edison bulbs.

Head south to **Urban Archaeology** (12), which is full of old shopfittings, stoneware and marble baths and sinks, door hardware, oversized lanterns and unusual industrial pieces. The majority of their stuff is made for warehouse/loft living. It is giant in scale!

On the same street is **Steven Alan** (13), which has a great interior — old shop fittings and cool industrial fittings. He makes a mean men's shirt and a fab selection of women's jewellery — plenty of fine gold — my personal favourite. Also stocks the best luggage in the world, out of Seattle, Filson. Here's the place to start any adventure. Oh, and the stripey cotton oversized towels are a must for $50. Hard to choose just one.

103

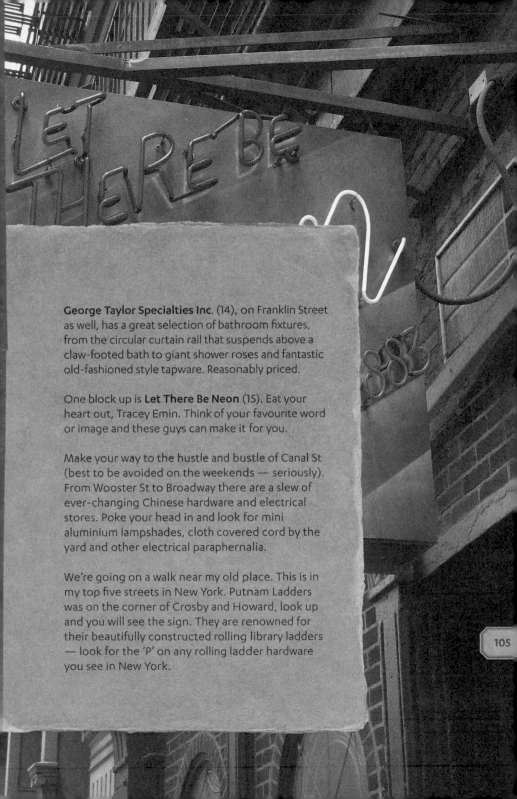

George Taylor Specialties Inc. (14), on Franklin Street as well, has a great selection of bathroom fixtures, from the circular curtain rail that suspends above a claw-footed bath to giant shower roses and fantastic old-fashioned style tapware. Reasonably priced.

One block up is **Let There Be Neon** (15). Eat your heart out, Tracey Emin. Think of your favourite word or image and these guys can make it for you.

Make your way to the hustle and bustle of Canal St (best to be avoided on the weekends — seriously). From Wooster St to Broadway there are a slew of ever-changing Chinese hardware and electrical stores. Poke your head in and look for mini aluminium lampshades, cloth covered cord by the yard and other electrical paraphernalia.

We're going on a walk near my old place. This is in my top five streets in New York. Putnam Ladders was on the corner of Crosby and Howard, look up and you will see the sign. They are renowned for their beautifully constructed rolling library ladders — look for the 'P' on any rolling ladder hardware you see in New York.

This corner is a hub. So you're going to check out **E. Vogel** (16). I have wanted a pair of their handmade riding boots FOREVER. They are continually on my Christmas and birthday list. They not only make riding boots, but also shoes to order.

Next is **Ted Muehling** (17). If you're feeling flat (actually if you're in any kind of mood), come here. Not only for his beautiful nature-inspired jewellery but also his coral-inspired spoons. The panelled walls are often pinned with dragonflies and sea creatures. I think my favourite window display of all time was the branch covered in migrating Monarch butterflies.

Then go to **BDDW** (18). For NYC and its limited space, I just love the grand scale of this. Big furniture and the choice of raw pieces of wood to make into your very own bespoke dining table. The styling of this shop is spectacular. Crazy things in crazy corners. For smaller packable items I love the wood banded mirror with leather strap.

Lefroy Brooks (19) is for when the bathroom is the show-off of your loft. Check out the all-black silver-claw-footed bath, classic tapware and even the handles of the giant showroom doors. Even their logo is fab.

Turn left on Broome and before Broadway, you will see **OK Hardware** (20). This was my local hardware store for 10 years. America still manufactures lots of its hardware onshore. So here you'll find canvas and leather, Klein tool bags, handmade brass nails (great for stretching canvases), brown paper stencils, Purdy paintbrushes, T-pins, and all the other cool, very American, items. I love American hardware stores.

Keep going on Broome to **Ochre** (21). Other than just being a drop dead gorgeous store, they have fantastic horn drawer pulls of all lengths and sizes. Owned by my friend Andrew. He makes it easy to decorate your own house without the need for an interior designer. Well-priced new upholstered pieces mixed in with vintage finds from America and Europe. His range of furniture, lighting, mirrors and hardware are displayed with fine porcelain, hand-blown glass, carved wood, Turkish towels, hand-forged scissors, and other necessities of life.

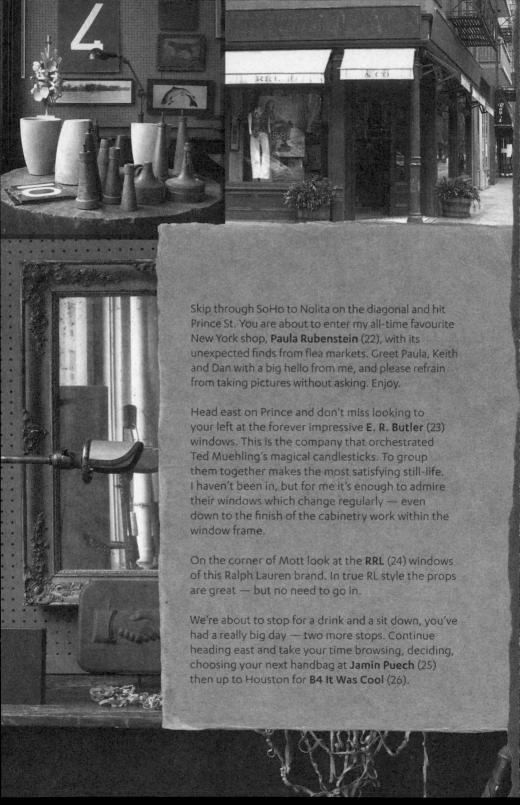

Skip through SoHo to Nolita on the diagonal and hit Prince St. You are about to enter my all-time favourite New York shop, **Paula Rubenstein** (22), with its unexpected finds from flea markets. Greet Paula, Keith and Dan with a big hello from me, and please refrain from taking pictures without asking. Enjoy.

Head east on Prince and don't miss looking to your left at the forever impressive **E. R. Butler** (23) windows. This is the company that orchestrated Ted Muehling's magical candlesticks. To group them together makes the most satisfying still-life. I haven't been in, but for me it's enough to admire their windows which change regularly — even down to the finish of the cabinetry work within the window frame.

On the corner of Mott look at the **RRL** (24) windows of this Ralph Lauren brand. In true RL style the props are great — but no need to go in.

We're about to stop for a drink and a sit down, you've had a really big day — two more stops. Continue heading east and take your time browsing, deciding, choosing your next handbag at **Jamin Puech** (25) then up to Houston for **B4 It Was Cool** (26).

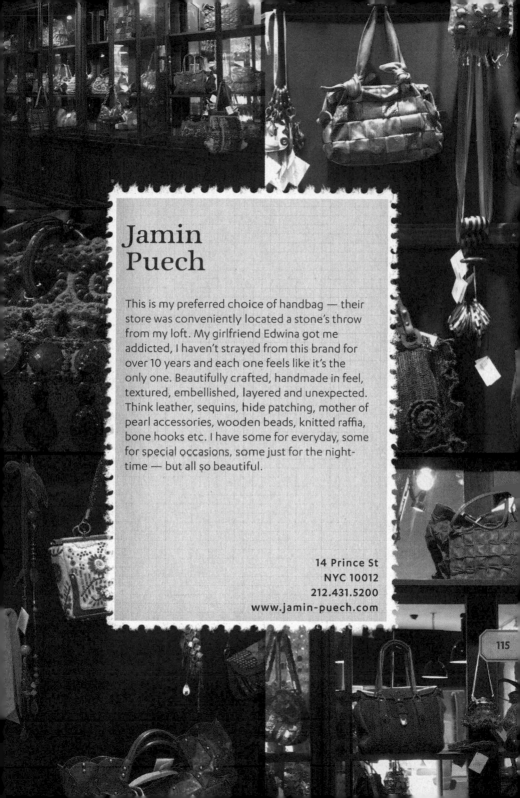

Jamin Puech

This is my preferred choice of handbag — their store was conveniently located a stone's throw from my loft. My girlfriend Edwina got me addicted, I haven't strayed from this brand for over 10 years and each one feels like it's the only one. Beautifully crafted, handmade in feel, textured, embellished, layered and unexpected. Think leather, sequins, hide patching, mother of pearl accessories, wooden beads, knitted raffia, bone hooks etc. I have some for everyday, some for special occasions, some just for the night-time — but all so beautiful.

**14 Prince St
NYC 10012
212.431.5200
www.jamin-puech.com**

B4
It Was
Cool

If you love vintage electrical as much as I do, this cave of MacGyver-style lights is awesome. Most of the parts are American-made, often in original form but also re-formatted. The owner, Gadi Gilan, takes a little warming up, but if he sees your passion, you'll be invited into the basement. Keep in mind, if you fall in love with as many things as I do, he will ship them to you. All you need are new lightbulbs, and a good electrician to change the plugs when you get home.

89 E. Houston St
NYC 10012
212.219.0139
www.b4itwascool.com

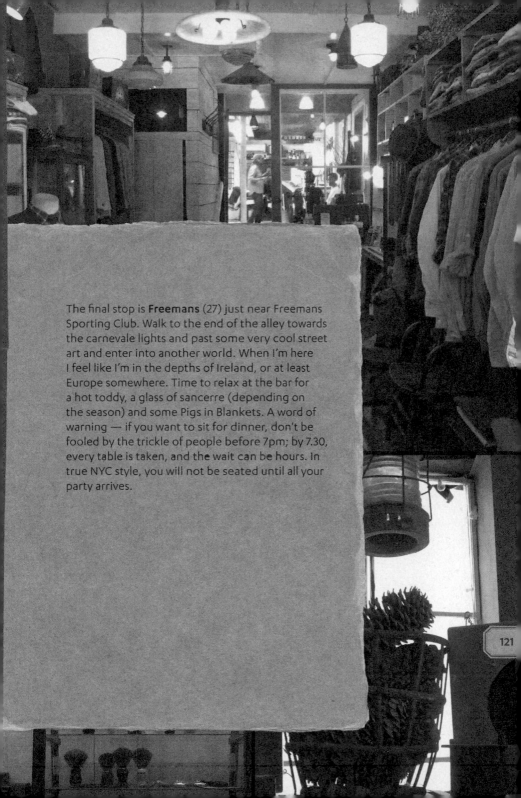

The final stop is **Freemans** (27) just near Freemans Sporting Club. Walk to the end of the alley towards the carnevale lights and past some very cool street art and enter into another world. When I'm here I feel like I'm in the depths of Ireland, or at least Europe somewhere. Time to relax at the bar for a hot toddy, a glass of sancerre (depending on the season) and some Pigs in Blankets. A word of warning — if you want to sit for dinner, don't be fooled by the trickle of people before 7pm; by 7.30, every table is taken, and the wait can be hours. In true NYC style, you will not be seated until all your party arrives.

haberd
&han

ashery
dmade

123

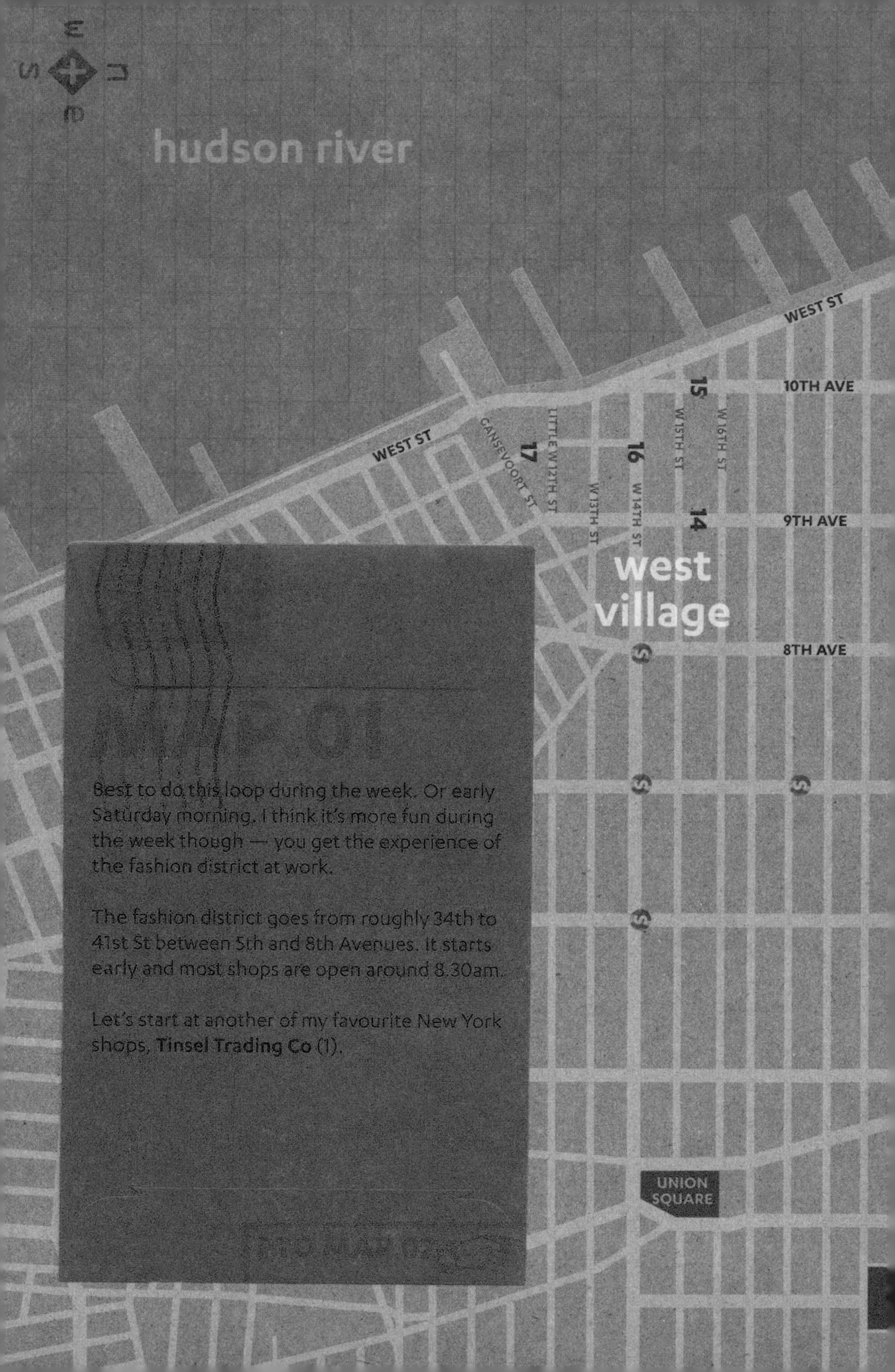

hudson river

WEST ST

WEST ST

GANSEVOORT ST

LITTLE W12TH ST

17

16

W13TH ST

W14TH ST

15

W15TH ST

W16TH ST

14

10TH AVE

9TH AVE

8TH AVE

west
village

$

$

$

$

UNION
SQUARE

Best to do this loop during the week. Or early
Saturday morning. I think it's more fun during
the week though — you get the experience of
the fashion district at work.

The fashion district goes from roughly 34th to
41st St between 5th and 8th Avenues. It starts
early and most shops are open around 8.30am.

Let's start at another of my favourite New York
shops, **Tinsel Trading Co (1)**.

MAP 01

MAP 02

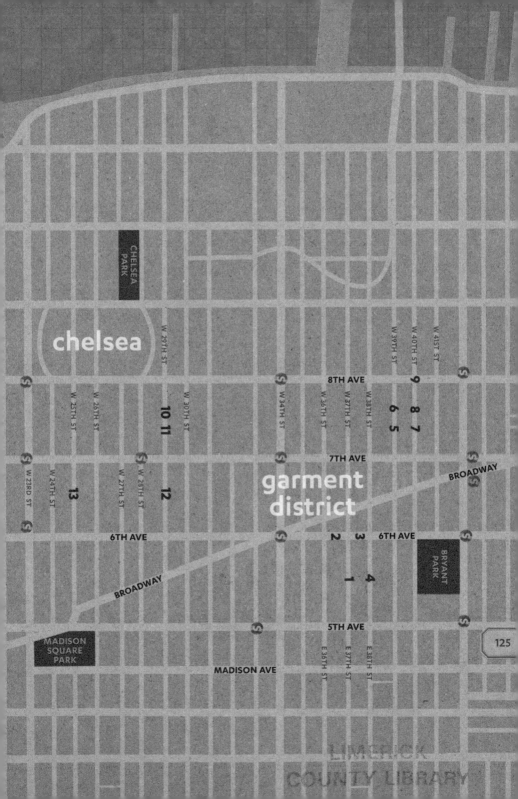

CHELSEA PARK

chelsea

W 29TH ST

W 25TH ST
W 26TH ST

W 30TH ST

10 11

W 23RD ST
W 24TH ST

13

W 27TH ST
W 28TH ST

12

6TH AVE

W 34TH ST

W 36TH ST
W 37TH ST
W 38TH ST

W 39TH ST
W 40TH ST
W 41ST ST

8TH AVE

9

6 8 7

5

7TH AVE

garment
district

BROADWAY

2 3 6TH AVE

1 4

BRYANT PARK

BROADWAY

5TH AVE

E 36TH ST
E 37TH ST
E 38TH ST

MADISON
SQUARE
PARK

MADISON AVE

FIBRE C

20 %
5 % ESSED WOOL
60 ON
10 ON
HER

Suite De la 6. Famille.

BALLSTO
KNITTIN

INDIGO BLUES

Sharing the love of my
favourite dye and textile.

* 45 rpm
* Liza Sherman
* Sri Threads
* Earnest Sewn
* Paula Rubenstein
* John Robshaw
* John Derian
* Chelsea Antiques Garage
* ABC Carpet & Home
* Amaridian
* Habu
* Kremer Pigments

hudson river

soho

tribeca

6TH AVE

SULLIVAN ST

THOMPSON ST

W BROADWAY

WOOSTER ST

CHURCH ST

CANAL ST

BROOME ST

SPRING ST

PRINCE ST

WEST HOUSTON ST

WASHINGTON SQUARE PARK

18
19
20

22

21

GREENE ST

23

MERCER ST

GRAND ST

BROADWAY

CROSBY ST

25

24

LAFAYETTE ST

LAFAYETTE ST

MULBERRY ST

MOTT ST

E 2ND ST

E 3RD ST

BOWERY

26

3RD AVE

E 4TH ST

E 5TH ST

little
italy

nolita

EAST HOUSTON ST

2ND AVE

east
village

SARA D ROOSEVELT PARK

127

Tinsel Trading Co

Marcia rules this store and frequently delves into the stock her grandfather amassed. Her story is fascinating — I recommend you read Kaari Meng's *Treasured Notions*, which gives you both a written and visual history. You might be aware of my fascination with all things haberdashery and hardware — well, this place totally satisfies the haberdashery side. Old-fashioned notions: velvet milliners' flowers, coloured feathers, scraps, glass glitter alphabet, metallic thread, giant tassels, ribbons, crepe paper flowers, passementerie, fringe, cards, buttons, garlands, ornaments and all other kinds of treasures. Notice the Putnam rolling ladder on the next page! (See also page 105.)

1 W. 37th St
NYC 10018
212.730.1030
www.tinseltrading.com

NEVERMORE!

129

131

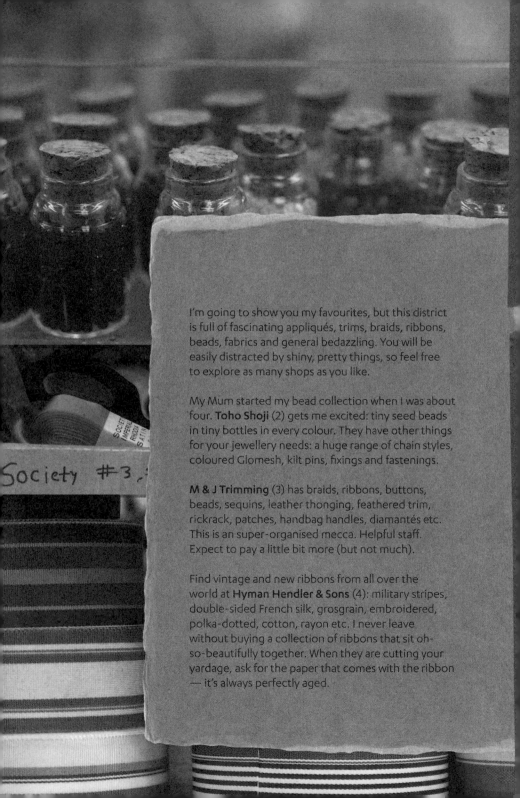

I'm going to show you my favourites, but this district is full of fascinating appliqués, trims, braids, ribbons, beads, fabrics and general bedazzling. You will be easily distracted by shiny, pretty things, so feel free to explore as many shops as you like.

My Mum started my bead collection when I was about four. **Toho Shoji** (2) gets me excited: tiny seed beads in tiny bottles in every colour. They have other things for your jewellery needs: a huge range of chain styles, coloured Glomesh, kilt pins, fixings and fastenings.

M & J Trimming (3) has braids, ribbons, buttons, beads, sequins, leather thonging, feathered trim, rickrack, patches, handbag handles, diamantés etc. This is an super-organised mecca. Helpful staff. Expect to pay a little bit more (but not much).

Find vintage and new ribbons from all over the world at **Hyman Hendler & Sons** (4): military stripes, double-sided French silk, grosgrain, embroidered, polka-dotted, cotton, rayon etc. I never leave without buying a collection of ribbons that sit oh-so-beautifully together. When they are cutting your yardage, ask for the paper that comes with the ribbon — it's always perfectly aged.

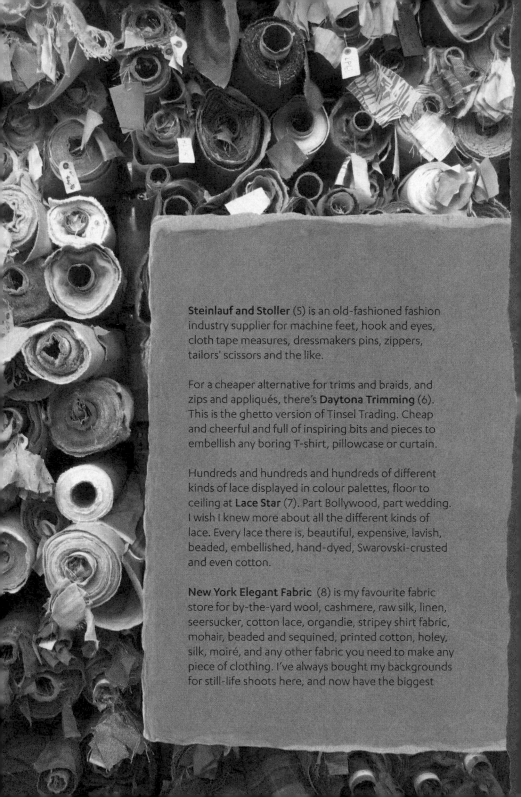

Steinlauf and Stoller (5) is an old-fashioned fashion industry supplier for machine feet, hook and eyes, cloth tape measures, dressmakers pins, zippers, tailors' scissors and the like.

For a cheaper alternative for trims and braids, and zips and appliqués, there's **Daytona Trimming** (6). This is the ghetto version of Tinsel Trading. Cheap and cheerful and full of inspiring bits and pieces to embellish any boring T-shirt, pillowcase or curtain.

Hundreds and hundreds and hundreds of different kinds of lace displayed in colour palettes, floor to ceiling at **Lace Star** (7). Part Bollywood, part wedding. I wish I knew more about all the different kinds of lace. Every lace there is, beautiful, expensive, lavish, beaded, embellished, hand-dyed, Swarovski-crusted and even cotton.

New York Elegant Fabric (8) is my favourite fabric store for by-the-yard wool, cashmere, raw silk, linen, seersucker, cotton lace, organdie, stripey shirt fabric, mohair, beaded and sequined, printed cotton, holey, silk, moiré, and any other fabric you need to make any piece of clothing. I've always bought my backgrounds for still-life shoots here, and now have the biggest

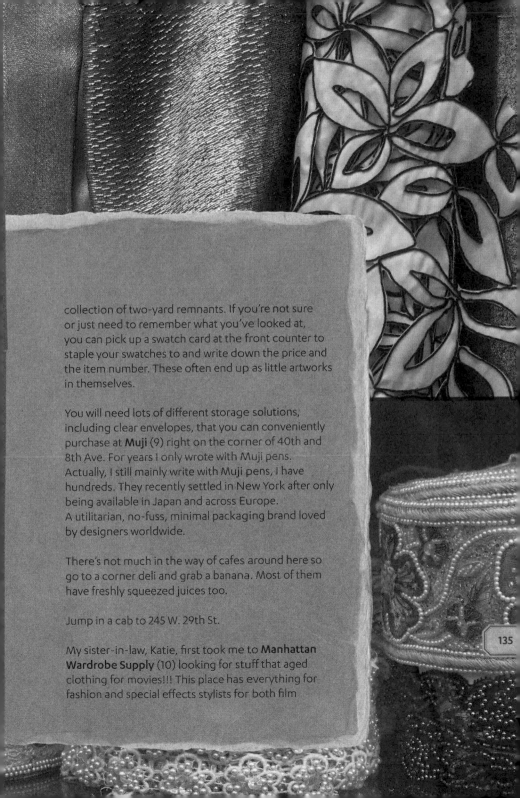

collection of two-yard remnants. If you're not sure or just need to remember what you've looked at, you can pick up a swatch card at the front counter to staple your swatches to and write down the price and the item number. These often end up as little artworks in themselves.

You will need lots of different storage solutions, including clear envelopes, that you can conveniently purchase at **Muji** (9) right on the corner of 40th and 8th Ave. For years I only wrote with Muji pens. Actually, I still mainly write with Muji pens, I have hundreds. They recently settled in New York after only being available in Japan and across Europe. A utilitarian, no-fuss, minimal packaging brand loved by designers worldwide.

There's not much in the way of cafes around here so go to a corner deli and grab a banana. Most of them have freshly squeezed juices too.

Jump in a cab to 245 W. 29th St.

My sister-in-law, Katie, first took me to **Manhattan Wardrobe Supply** (10) looking for stuff that aged clothing for movies!!! This place has everything for fashion and special effects stylists for both film

135

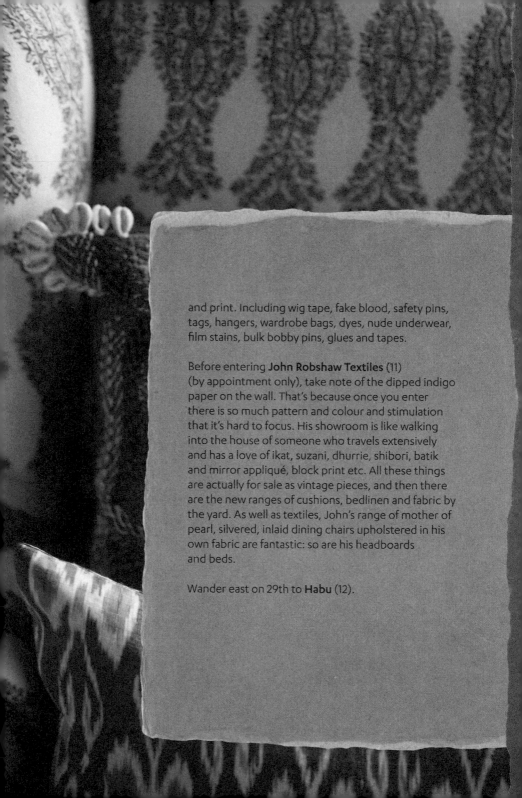

and print. Including wig tape, fake blood, safety pins, tags, hangers, wardrobe bags, dyes, nude underwear, film stains, bulk bobby pins, glues and tapes.

Before entering **John Robshaw Textiles** (11) (by appointment only), take note of the dipped indigo paper on the wall. That's because once you enter there is so much pattern and colour and stimulation that it's hard to focus. His showroom is like walking into the house of someone who travels extensively and has a love of ikat, suzani, dhurrie, shibori, batik and mirror appliqué, block print etc. All these things are actually for sale as vintage pieces, and then there are the new ranges of cushions, bedlinen and fabric by the yard. As well as textiles, John's range of mother of pearl, silvered, inlaid dining chairs upholstered in his own fabric are fantastic: so are his headboards and beds.

Wander east on 29th to **Habu** (12).

Habu

This is one of those hidden gems in an office block in New York. All things natural, all things fibre from across Asia, that can be used for weaving, knitting, crochet and the like. It's not only wool. Even dried silk cocoons. You can buy a sample book of all their fibres for $27. There's a small selection of ready-made objects; I bought a knotted coin purse and scarf made from Laotian fibre.

135 W. 29th St #804
NYC 10001
212.239.3546
www.habutextiles.com

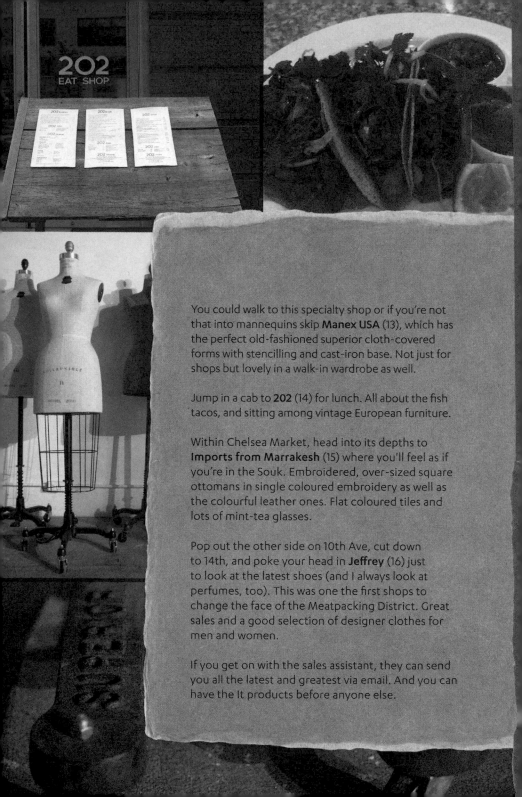

You could walk to this specialty shop or if you're not that into mannequins skip **Manex USA** (13), which has the perfect old-fashioned superior cloth-covered forms with stencilling and cast-iron base. Not just for shops but lovely in a walk-in wardrobe as well.

Jump in a cab to **202** (14) for lunch. All about the fish tacos, and sitting among vintage European furniture.

Within Chelsea Market, head into its depths to **Imports from Marrakesh** (15) where you'll feel as if you're in the Souk. Embroidered, over-sized square ottomans in single coloured embroidery as well as the colourful leather ones. Flat coloured tiles and lots of mint-tea glasses.

Pop out the other side on 10th Ave, cut down to 14th, and poke your head in **Jeffrey** (16) just to look at the latest shoes (and I always look at perfumes, too). This was one the first shops to change the face of the Meatpacking District. Great sales and a good selection of designer clothes for men and women.

If you get on with the sales assistant, they can send you all the latest and greatest via email. And you can have the It products before anyone else.

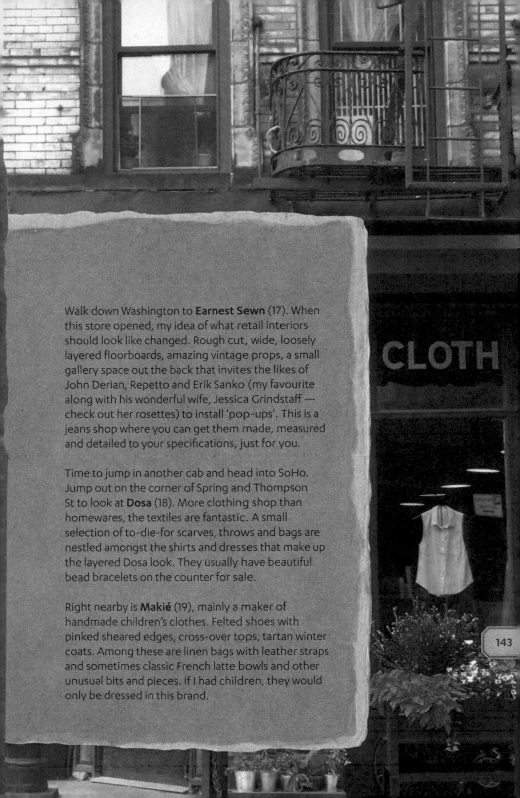

Walk down Washington to **Earnest Sewn** (17). When this store opened, my idea of what retail interiors should look like changed. Rough cut, wide, loosely layered floorboards, amazing vintage props, a small gallery space out the back that invites the likes of John Derian, Repetto and Erik Sanko (my favourite along with his wonderful wife, Jessica Grindstaff — check out her rosettes) to install 'pop-ups'. This is a jeans shop where you can get them made, measured and detailed to your specifications, just for you.

Time to jump in another cab and head into SoHo. Jump out on the corner of Spring and Thompson St to look at **Dosa** (18). More clothing shop than homewares, the textiles are fantastic. A small selection of to-die-for scarves, throws and bags are nestled amongst the shirts and dresses that make up the layered Dosa look. They usually have beautiful bead bracelets on the counter for sale.

Right nearby is **Makié** (19), mainly a maker of handmade children's clothes. Felted shoes with pinked sheared edges, cross-over tops, tartan winter coats. Among these are linen bags with leather straps and sometimes classic French latte bowls and other unusual bits and pieces. If I had children, they would only be dressed in this brand.

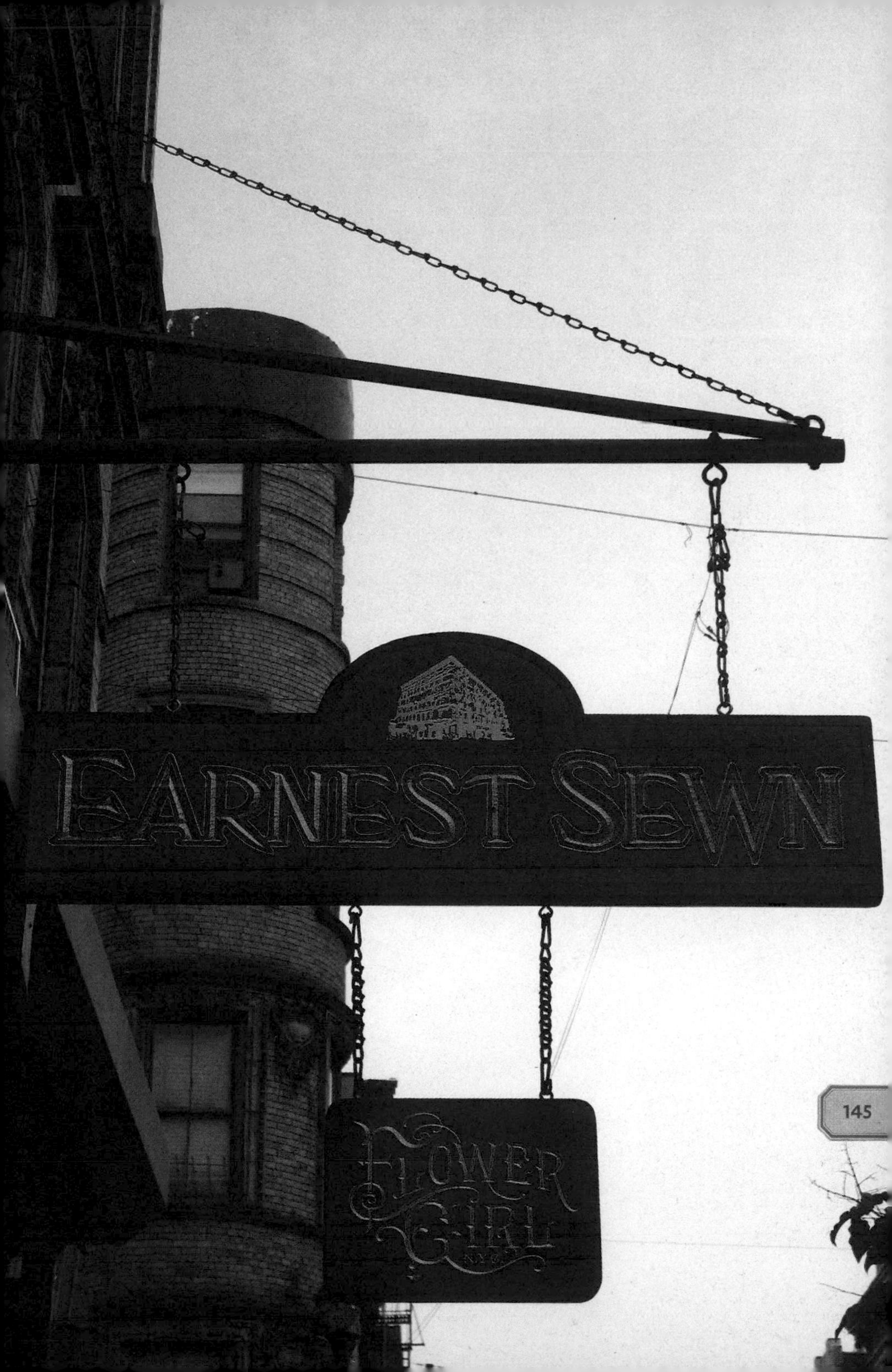
EARNEST SEWN
FLOWER
GIRL

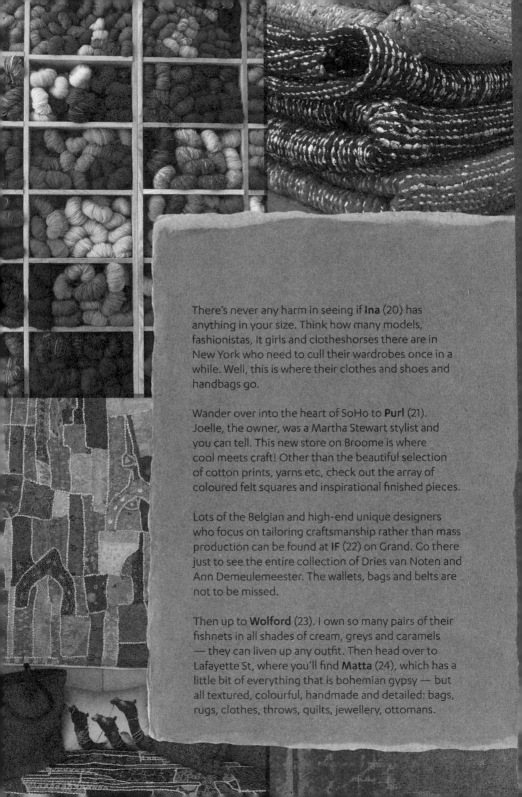

There's never any harm in seeing if **Ina** (20) has anything in your size. Think how many models, fashionistas, It girls and clotheshorses there are in New York who need to cull their wardrobes once in a while. Well, this is where their clothes and shoes and handbags go.

Wander over into the heart of SoHo to **Purl** (21). Joelle, the owner, was a Martha Stewart stylist and you can tell. This new store on Broome is where cool meets craft! Other than the beautiful selection of cotton prints, yarns etc, check out the array of coloured felt squares and inspirational finished pieces.

Lots of the Belgian and high-end unique designers who focus on tailoring craftsmanship rather than mass production can be found at **IF** (22) on Grand. Go there just to see the entire collection of Dries van Noten and Ann Demeulemeester. The wallets, bags and belts are not to be missed.

Then up to **Wolford** (23). I own so many pairs of their fishnets in all shades of cream, greys and caramels — they can liven up any outfit. Then head over to Lafayette St, where you'll find **Matta** (24), which has a little bit of everything that is bohemian gypsy — but all textured, colourful, handmade and detailed: bags, rugs, clothes, throws, quilts, jewellery, ottomans.

147

It's a walk from there to the next two possibilities.
Finish off the day:
1. with freshly shucked oysters and a glass of
champagne at the zinc-topped bar at **Balthazar** (25),
or, if you're lucky, they serve boiled eggs around 4pm.

or

2. if you happen to have a stylist friend who can help
you gain access to **Albright Fashion Library** (26),
you'll be able to rent the latest, the greatest, the
most glamorous frock in New York for whatever
do you've been invited to. This is what it would
be like to walk into Carrie Bradshaw and Patricia
Field's wardrobes combined. A huge loft that has
no furniture — only clothing racks and shoe racks,
all colour coordinated.

dra
uph

pers &
olstery

151

N
W E
S

hudson river

LEROY ST
CLARKSON ST
GREENWICH ST
HUDSON ST
11

west
village

greenwich
village

soho

W BROADWAY
BROOME ST
WOOSTER ST
GREENE ST
SPRING ST
18
17
MERCER ST
GRAND ST
BROADWAY
CROSBY ST
LAFAYETTE ST
16
14
15
CENTRE ST

little
italy

DELANCEY ST
BROOME ST
13

WEST HOUSTON ST
PRINCE ST
20
12
LAFAYETTE ST
MULBERRY ST
MOTT ST
ELIZABETH ST
BOWERY

nolita

WASHINGTON
SQUARE PARK

BLEECKER ST

BROADWAY

UNIVERSITY PL
W 11TH ST
E 9TH ST
E 10TH ST
10
E 11TH ST

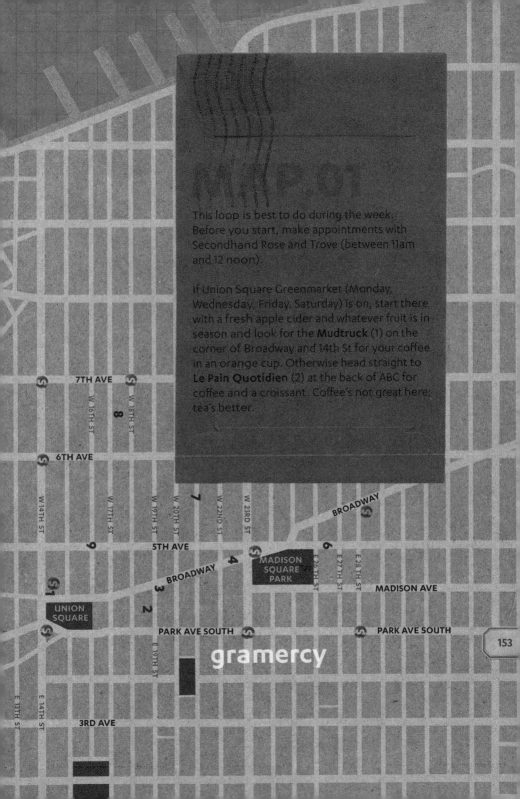

This loop is best to do during the week. Before you start, make appointments with Secondhand Rose and Trove (between 11am and 12 noon).

If Union Square Greenmarket (Monday, Wednesday, Friday, Saturday) is on, start there with a fresh apple cider and whatever fruit is in season and look for the **Mudtruck** (1) on the corner of Broadway and 14th St for your coffee in an orange cup. Otherwise head straight to **Le Pain Quotidien** (2) at the back of ABC for coffee and a croissant. Coffee's not great here; tea's better.

7TH AVE

8

W 16TH ST

W 18TH ST

6TH AVE

W 14TH ST

W 17TH ST

W 19TH ST

W 20TH ST

7

W 22ND ST

W 23RD ST

BROADWAY

5TH AVE

9

4

MADISON
SQUARE
PARK

E 26TH ST

9

E 27TH ST

E 28TH ST

MADISON AVE

3

BROADWAY

2

UNION
SQUARE

PARK AVE SOUTH

PARK AVE SOUTH

E 19TH ST

gramercy

E 13TH ST

E 14TH ST

3RD AVE

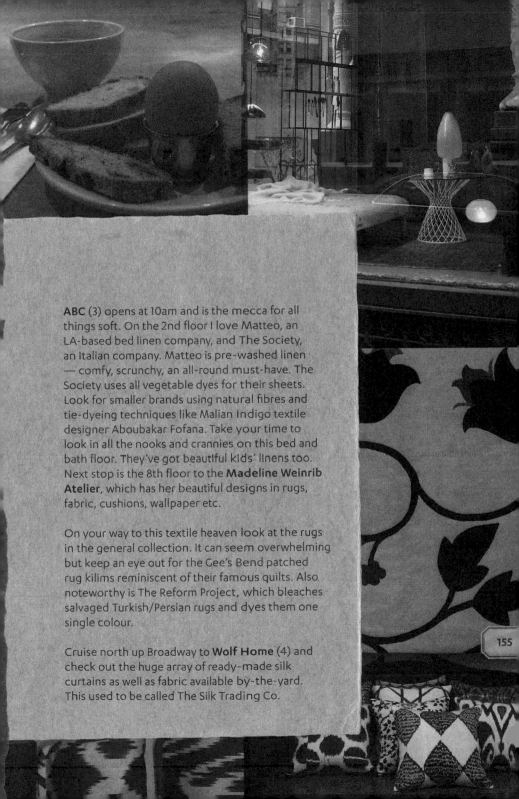

ABC (3) opens at 10am and is the mecca for all things soft. On the 2nd floor I love Matteo, an LA-based bed linen company, and The Society, an Italian company. Matteo is pre-washed linen — comfy, scrunchy, an all-round must-have. The Society uses all vegetable dyes for their sheets. Look for smaller brands using natural fibres and tie-dyeing techniques like Malian Indigo textile designer Aboubakar Fofana. Take your time to look in all the nooks and crannies on this bed and bath floor. They've got beautiful kids' linens too. Next stop is the 8th floor to the **Madeline Weinrib Atelier**, which has her beautiful designs in rugs, fabric, cushions, wallpaper etc.

On your way to this textile heaven look at the rugs in the general collection. It can seem overwhelming but keep an eye out for the Gee's Bend patched rug kilims reminiscent of their famous quilts. Also noteworthy is The Reform Project, which bleaches salvaged Turkish/Persian rugs and dyes them one single colour.

Cruise north up Broadway to **Wolf Home** (4) and check out the huge array of ready-made silk curtains as well as fabric available by-the-yard. This used to be called The Silk Trading Co.

157

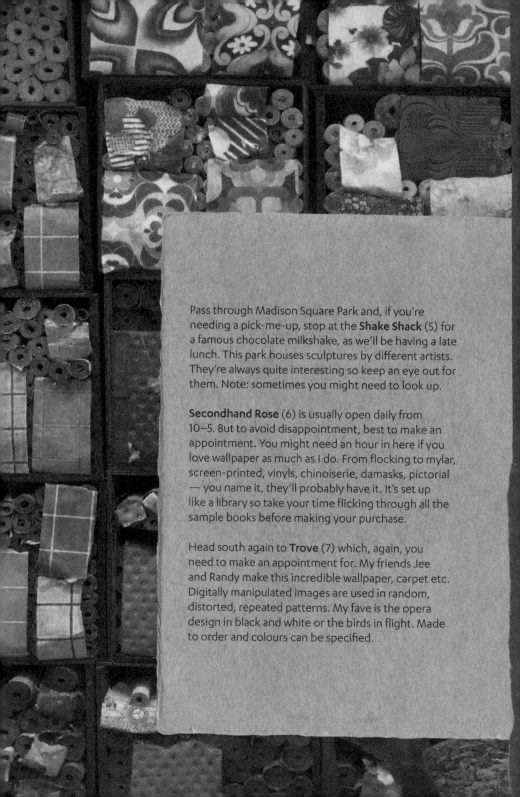

Pass through Madison Square Park and, if you're needing a pick-me-up, stop at the **Shake Shack** (5) for a famous chocolate milkshake, as we'll be having a late lunch. This park houses sculptures by different artists. They're always quite interesting so keep an eye out for them. Note: sometimes you might need to look up.

Secondhand Rose (6) is usually open daily from 10–5. But to avoid disappointment, best to make an appointment. You might need an hour in here if you love wallpaper as much as I do. From flocking to mylar, screen-printed, vinyls, chinoiserie, damasks, pictorial — you name it, they'll probably have it. It's set up like a library so take your time flicking through all the sample books before making your purchase.

Head south again to **Trove** (7) which, again, you need to make an appointment for. My friends Jee and Randy make this incredible wallpaper, carpet etc. Digitally manipulated images are used in random, distorted, repeated patterns. My fave is the opera design in black and white or the birds in flight. Made to order and colours can be specified.

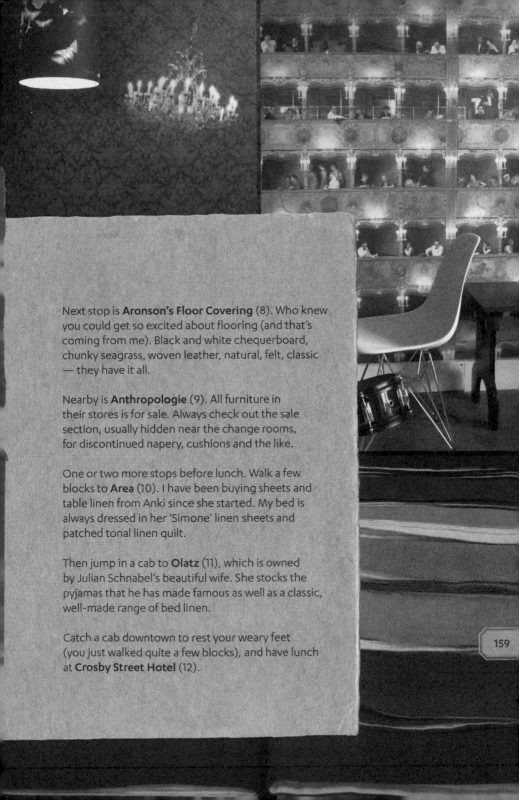

Next stop is **Aronson's Floor Covering** (8). Who knew you could get so excited about flooring (and that's coming from me). Black and white chequerboard, chunky seagrass, woven leather, natural, felt, classic — they have it all.

Nearby is **Anthropologie** (9). All furniture in their stores is for sale. Always check out the sale section, usually hidden near the change rooms, for discontinued napery, cushions and the like.

One or two more stops before lunch. Walk a few blocks to **Area** (10). I have been buying sheets and table linen from Anki since she started. My bed is always dressed in her 'Simone' linen sheets and patched tonal linen quilt.

Then jump in a cab to **Olatz** (11), which is owned by Julian Schnabel's beautiful wife. She stocks the pyjamas that he has made famous as well as a classic, well-made range of bed linen.

Catch a cab downtown to rest your weary feet (you just walked quite a few blocks), and have lunch at **Crosby Street Hotel** (12).

Crosby Street Hotel

Kit Kemp designed this hotel, and it really feels like an extension of someone's home, with its carefully selected pieces and art from an educated eye. If you have the opportunity to stay here, you have access to the library and honesty bar as well as the fantastic outdoor courtyard with faux bois furniture. Otherwise, after checking out the foyer and adjoining rooms, and admiring the amazing textiles, space and furniture, have a well-deserved lunch in the restaurant.

79 Crosby St
NYC 10012
212.226.6400
www.firmdale.com

Walk east on Spring St to **Just Shades** (13), where every lampshade imaginable is pretty much available off the shelf. If you want your own shape and choice of fabric, they will custom make it for you. Then walk south on Elizabeth to Broome St and head towards SoHo. You've got a few stops on the way.

First up is **Canvas** (14), a spin-off from Ochre, with its buttoned sailcloth chesterfields, Syrian glassware, handthrown porcelain, cushions, throws and other lovely tactile pieces.

Next is **Calypso Home** (15). This corner at Lafayette and Broome is locally known as Calypso Corner, due to the abundance of Calypso stores: clothing, kidsware, sale shop, candles, jewellery etc.

Then Thomas O'Brien's **Aero** (16), which is full of serious grown-up interior pieces with not-so-serious tabletop. Very tonal muted palettes set up in a variety of vistas. He has his own range of furniture and lighting mixed in with other brands. I had the chance to go downstairs and it is unexpectedly huge, with lots of staff designing furniture, spaces, products etc etc. So when you're walking around, know that there's a hive of creativity beneath you.

Next we're off to **Jonathan Adler** (17) on Greene St.

Jonathan
Adler

For years, I have featured his work in magazines around the world — lacquered tables, velvet chairs, ceramic tabletop range, neat lounges, tapestry cushions, original udder vases, as well as his own house. Other than his very well priced furniture, check out his new wallpaper range — knots, faux bamboo and Greek key are my favourites. He absolutely owns this look: so Palm Springs, oh-so-fabulous! Always tongue-in-cheek and with a sense of humour.

47 Greene St
NYC 10013
212.941.8950
www.jonathanadler.com

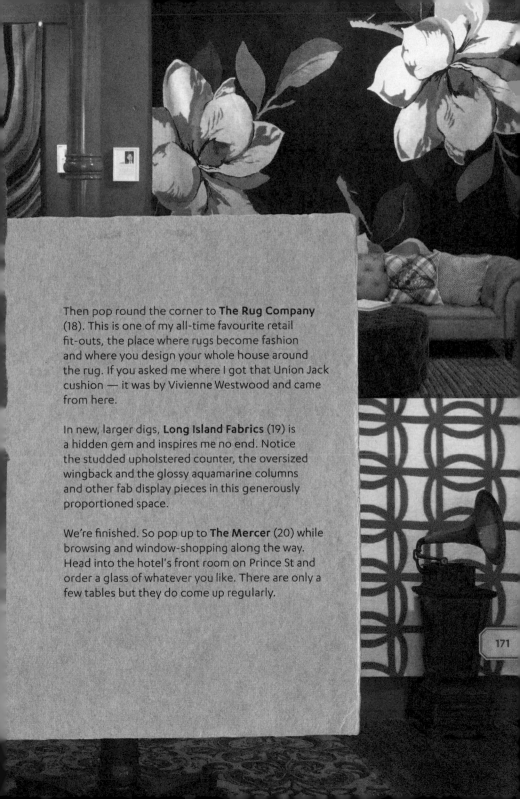

Then pop round the corner to **The Rug Company** (18). This is one of my all-time favourite retail fit-outs, the place where rugs become fashion and where you design your whole house around the rug. If you asked me where I got that Union Jack cushion — it was by Vivienne Westwood and came from here.

In new, larger digs, **Long Island Fabrics** (19) is a hidden gem and inspires me no end. Notice the studded upholstered counter, the oversized wingback and the glossy aquamarine columns and other fab display pieces in this generously proportioned space.

We're finished. So pop up to **The Mercer** (20) while browsing and window-shopping along the way. Head into the hotel's front room on Prince St and order a glass of whatever you like. There are only a few tables but they do come up regularly.

art &
objets

173

central park

THE
LAKE

JACQUELINE KENNEDY
ONASSIS RESERVOIR

5TH AVE

MADISON AVE

PARK AVE

1 E 91ST ST

2 E 89TH ST

E 88TH ST

E 87TH ST

E 90TH ST

upper
east side

Frustratingly, some parts of New York open
a bit late. So for this loop you can sleep in or
take your time over breakfast.

This loop is a big one — don't feel you need to
do it in a day. I'm going to give you two places
for lunch. Chelsea isn't open on Mondays, so
best to do Tuesday through Saturday.

DAY 1
Ring **BG**, the Kelly Wearstler designed
restaurant on the 7th floor of Bergdorf
Goodman, the famous department store.
If possible, book table 1 or 2. It's all loveliness
(this is for lunch).

N E S W

hudson river

HOLLAND TUNNEL

west
village

GREENWICH ST

HUDSON ST

GREENWICH ST

14

RENWICK ST

SPRING ST

VANDAM ST

HUDSON ST

CANAL ST

VARICK ST

soho

6TH AVE

SULLIVAN ST

THOMPSON ST

WASHINGTON
SQUARE PARK

BROOME ST

SPRING ST

PRINCE ST

WEST HOUSTON ST

WOOSTER ST

CANAL ST

GREENE ST

GRAND ST

MERCER ST

15

16

BLEECKER ST

BROADWAY

BROADWAY

17

CROSBY ST

LAFAYETTE ST

18 19

CENTRE ST

HOWARD ST

LAFAYETTE ST

22 23 24

26 27

E 2ND ST

BOWERY

25

little
italy

MULBERRY ST

DELANCY ST

MOTT ST

20 21

ELIZABETH ST

E 1ST ST

E 3RD ST

E 4TH ST

E 5TH ST

nolita

BOWERY

EAST HOUSTON ST

CHRYSTIE ST

SARA D ROOSEVELT PARK

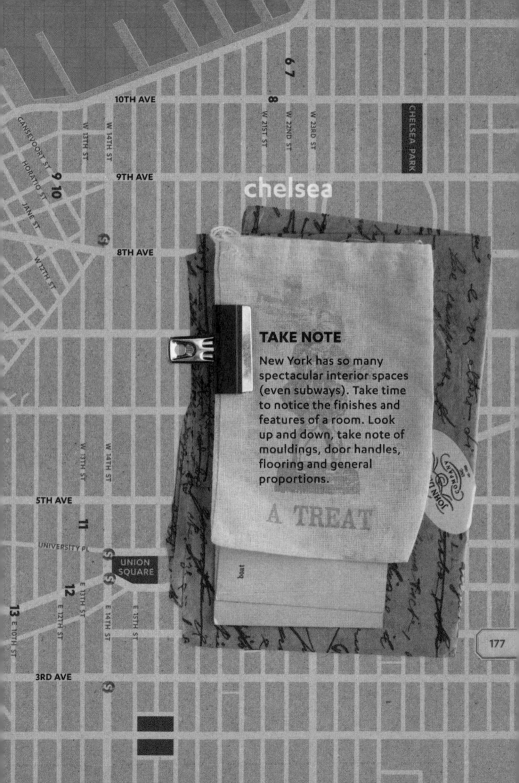

TAKE NOTE

New York has so many spectacular interior spaces (even subways). Take time to notice the finishes and features of a room. Look up and down, take note of mouldings, door handles, flooring and general proportions.

A TREAT

BG

I happened to be propping (definition of someone paying you to shop) on the day BG opened. It would have been rude not to have stopped. I sat at the beautiful green stone bar overlooking Central Park, was served perfectly chilled rose champagne by the friendliest of barmen and admired the incredible setting that Kelly Wearstler had created. It was mid-afternoon and was a favourite New York moment.

at Bergdorf Goodman
7th fl. 754 5th Ave
NYC 10019

179

Let's start at a museum. The **Cooper-Hewitt** (1) opens at 10. It's a design-based museum, with revolving exhibitions by guest curators who are always very interesting people. Not necessarily big designers, but always someone you want to know about. These people get the treat of exploring CH's vast archives and choosing whatever they like to make up their themed exhibition.

From there, walk past the **Guggenheim** (2), just to see the building — it's awe-inspiring even if you're not interested in what's showing at the time. Jump in a cab to 59th St and 5th Ave. The Plaza — it's always fun to look in the Palm Court and the Oak Room before you go to **Assouline** (3). There are two great publishers that just focus on fashion, photography, design and art, and this is one of them. Not only do they sell beautiful books, but they have a range of objets, my favourite being the 'e' ostrich egg.

When you've had enough of book browsing, head across the road to **Bergdorf Goodman** (4). The 5th Ave windows are a must-see before you head to the 7th floor.

181

LIVING WITH
WHAT YOU LOVE

Bergdorf Goodman

Go here for house and home accessories. A huge range of all the classic tabletop, stemware and flatware brands (reads like a bridal registry!) as well as vintage silver, books, stationery, fancy kitchen equipment, handblown vases, scented candles, Murano glass, French porcelain, decoupage, sugarcubes with flowers, candy bowls, Kelly Wearstler objets d'art designed especially for BG, and everything else you need for your Bahamas retreat, East Hampton weekender, NY brownstone and upstate estate. You might take a little while making your way to your pre-booked table at BG.

754 5th Ave
NYC 10019
212.753.7300
www.bergdorfgoodman.com

185

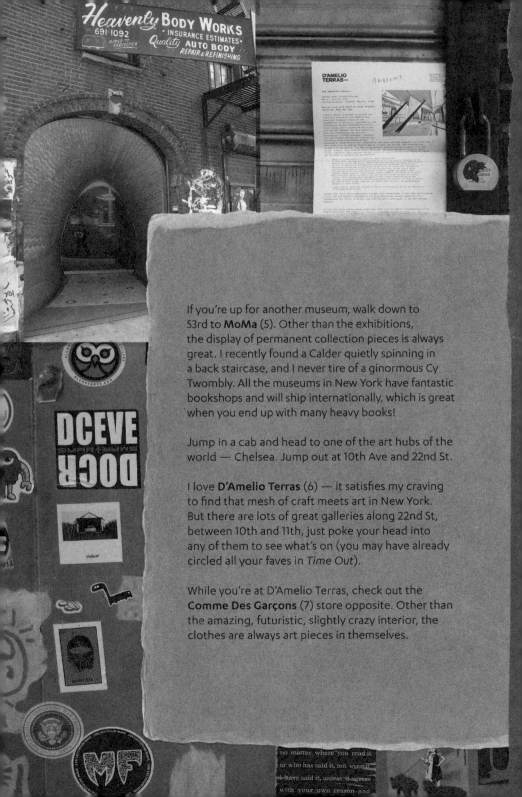

If you're up for another museum, walk down to 53rd to **MoMa** (5). Other than the exhibitions, the display of permanent collection pieces is always great. I recently found a Calder quietly spinning in a back staircase, and I never tire of a ginormous Cy Twombly. All the museums in New York have fantastic bookshops and will ship internationally, which is great when you end up with many heavy books!

Jump in a cab and head to one of the art hubs of the world — Chelsea. Jump out at 10th Ave and 22nd St.

I love **D'Amelio Terras** (6) — it satisfies my craving to find that mesh of craft meets art in New York. But there are lots of great galleries along 22nd St, between 10th and 11th, just poke your head into any of them to see what's on (you may have already circled all your faves in *Time Out*).

While you're at D'Amelio Terras, check out the **Comme Des Garçons** (7) store opposite. Other than the amazing, futuristic, slightly crazy interior, the clothes are always art pieces in themselves.

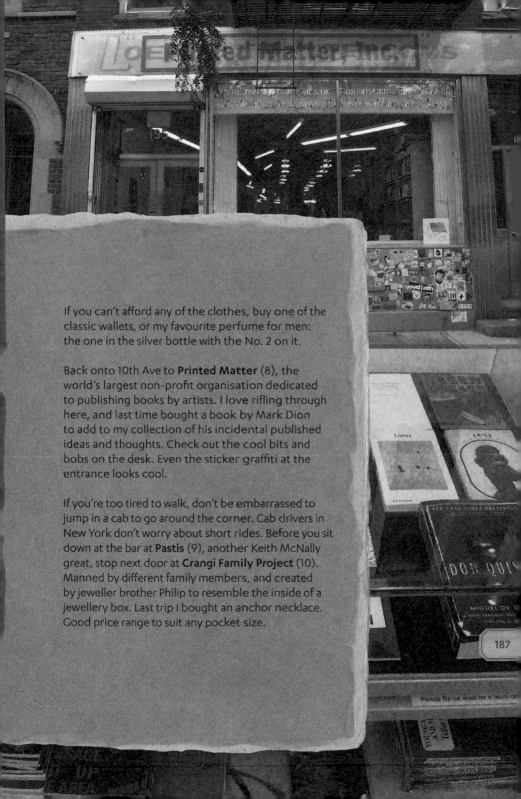

If you can't afford any of the clothes, buy one of the classic wallets, or my favourite perfume for men: the one in the silver bottle with the No. 2 on it.

Back onto 10th Ave to **Printed Matter** (8), the world's largest non-profit organisation dedicated to publishing books by artists. I love rifling through here, and last time bought a book by Mark Dion to add to my collection of his incidental published ideas and thoughts. Check out the cool bits and bobs on the desk. Even the sticker graffiti at the entrance looks cool.

If you're too tired to walk, don't be embarrassed to jump in a cab to go around the corner. Cab drivers in New York don't worry about short rides. Before you sit down at the bar at **Pastis** (9), another Keith McNally great, stop next door at **Crangi Family Project** (10). Manned by different family members, and created by jeweller brother Philip to resemble the inside of a jewellery box. Last trip I bought an anchor necklace. Good price range to suit any pocket size.

DAY 2
Hopefully, you'll have had a restful sleep, and pick up where you left off. It's all downtown. Grab coffee at the 13th St outpost of **Joe's** (11) and then wander over to Broadway to **The Strand** (12), which opens at 9.30. I go straight to Level 2 to the art, design, photography and travel books. If you're into rare books, they have a section next door. Just ask at information to be pointed in the right direction.

If you wander down Broadway, you'll come across **Broadway Windows** (13), which wraps the corner of Broadway and 10th St. You can't go in, and it's open all hours. These are literally windows which display one artist at one time. The art sits mostly in that blurry division between art and craft.

Catch a cab down Broadway to **Wyeth** (14). It is strictly by appointment, but if you're serious about design they have an incredible selection of objets and furniture. It's pricey but it's unusual, it's vintage, it's fabulous.

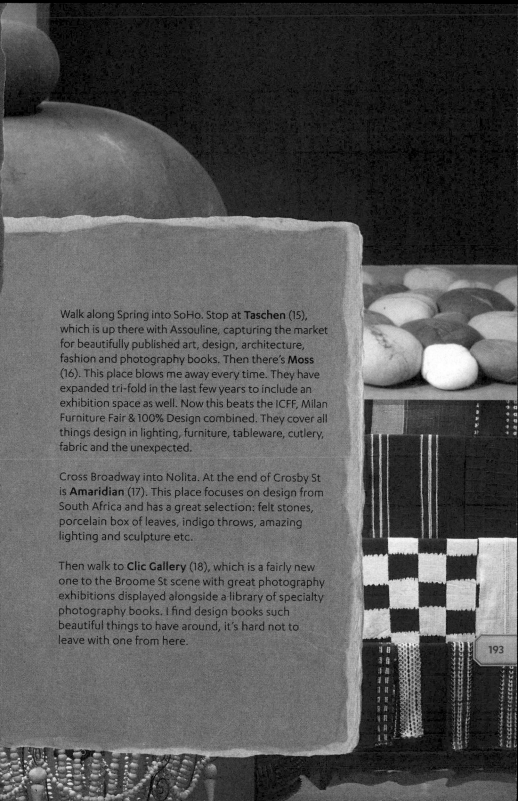

Walk along Spring into SoHo. Stop at **Taschen** (15), which is up there with Assouline, capturing the market for beautifully published art, design, architecture, fashion and photography books. Then there's **Moss** (16). This place blows me away every time. They have expanded tri-fold in the last few years to include an exhibition space as well. Now this beats the ICFF, Milan Furniture Fair & 100% Design combined. They cover all things design in lighting, furniture, tableware, cutlery, fabric and the unexpected.

Cross Broadway into Nolita. At the end of Crosby St is **Amaridian** (17). This place focuses on design from South Africa and has a great selection: felt stones, porcelain box of leaves, indigo throws, amazing lighting and sculpture etc.

Then walk to **Clic Gallery** (18), which is a fairly new one to the Broome St scene with great photography exhibitions displayed alongside a library of specialty photography books. I find design books such beautiful things to have around, it's hard not to leave with one from here.

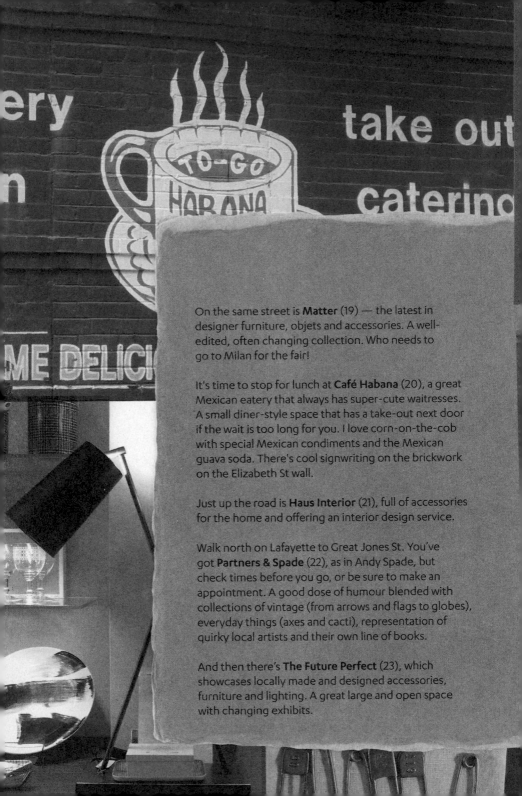

On the same street is **Matter** (19) — the latest in designer furniture, objets and accessories. A well-edited, often changing collection. Who needs to go to Milan for the fair!

It's time to stop for lunch at **Café Habana** (20), a great Mexican eatery that always has super-cute waitresses. A small diner-style space that has a take-out next door if the wait is too long for you. I love corn-on-the-cob with special Mexican condiments and the Mexican guava soda. There's cool signwriting on the brickwork on the Elizabeth St wall.

Just up the road is **Haus Interior** (21), full of accessories for the home and offering an interior design service.

Walk north on Lafayette to Great Jones St. You've got **Partners & Spade** (22), as in Andy Spade, but check times before you go, or be sure to make an appointment. A good dose of humour blended with collections of vintage (from arrows and flags to globes), everyday things (axes and cacti), representation of quirky local artists and their own line of books.

And then there's **The Future Perfect** (23), which showcases locally made and designed accessories, furniture and lighting. A great large and open space with changing exhibits.

separately

BELL HELMETS

The Choice of Professionals

195

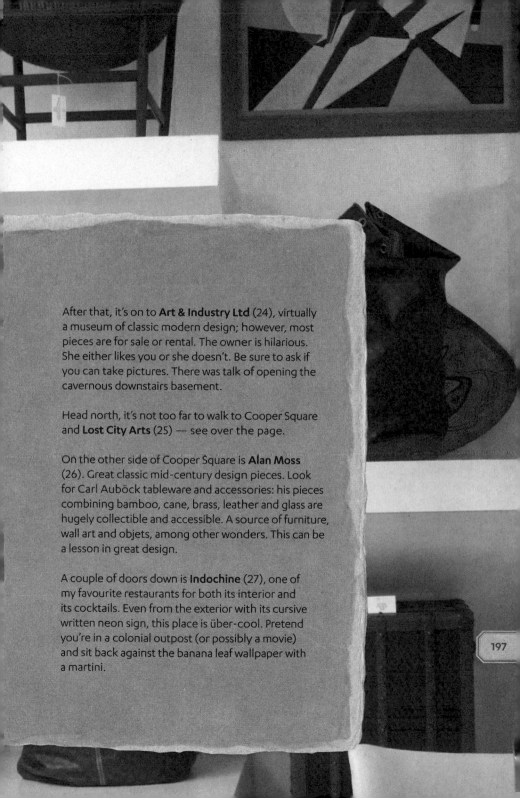

After that, it's on to **Art & Industry Ltd** (24), virtually a museum of classic modern design; however, most pieces are for sale or rental. The owner is hilarious. She either likes you or she doesn't. Be sure to ask if you can take pictures. There was talk of opening the cavernous downstairs basement.

Head north, it's not too far to walk to Cooper Square and **Lost City Arts** (25) — see over the page.

On the other side of Cooper Square is **Alan Moss** (26). Great classic mid-century design pieces. Look for Carl Auböck tableware and accessories: his pieces combining bamboo, cane, brass, leather and glass are hugely collectible and accessible. A source of furniture, wall art and objets, among other wonders. This can be a lesson in great design.

A couple of doors down is **Indochine** (27), one of my favourite restaurants for both its interior and its cocktails. Even from the exterior with its cursive written neon sign, this place is über-cool. Pretend you're in a colonial outpost (or possibly a movie) and sit back against the banana leaf wallpaper with a martini.

Lost
City
Arts

Original Arne Jacobsen, Calder, Hans Wegner,
Bertoia, Knoll and the like. Beautiful pieces
for stand-alone or to mix in with your existing
collection. If the furniture is out of reach, there is
always an interesting selection of wall art, mobiles
and objets. Owner Jim has had a long-time love
affair with the works of Bertoia. Unlike the famous
metal chairs we all know and respect, Bertoia
actually devoted most of his life to making beautiful
outdoor 'singing' sculptures. The sounds they
make, from giant gongs to wavy grass-like ones,
are like sirens' songs.

18 Cooper Square
NYC 10003
212.375.0500
www.lostcityarts.com

199

p

art

s

aper&

upplies

201

hudson river

HUDSON ST

7TH AVE

GREENWICH ST

CHARLTON ST

15

VANDAM ST

CANAL ST

VARICK ST

6TH AVE

tribeca

SULLIVAN ST

THOMPSON ST

soho

WORTH ST

LEONARD ST

FRANKLIN ST

1

W BROADWAY

BROOME ST

SPRING ST

16

WEST HOUSTON ST

BLEECKER ST

CHURCH ST

WOOSTER ST

4

GREENE ST

PRINCE ST

2

WHITE ST

3

MERCER ST

17

23

BROADWAY

22

BROADWAY

GRAND ST

18

21 **19**

CROSBY ST

20

HOWARD ST

LAFAYETTE ST

LAFAYETTE ST

CANAL ST

little
italy

MULBERRY ST

PRINCE ST

MOTT ST

SPRING ST

nolita

2ND AVE

SARA D ROOSEVELT PARK

1ST AVE

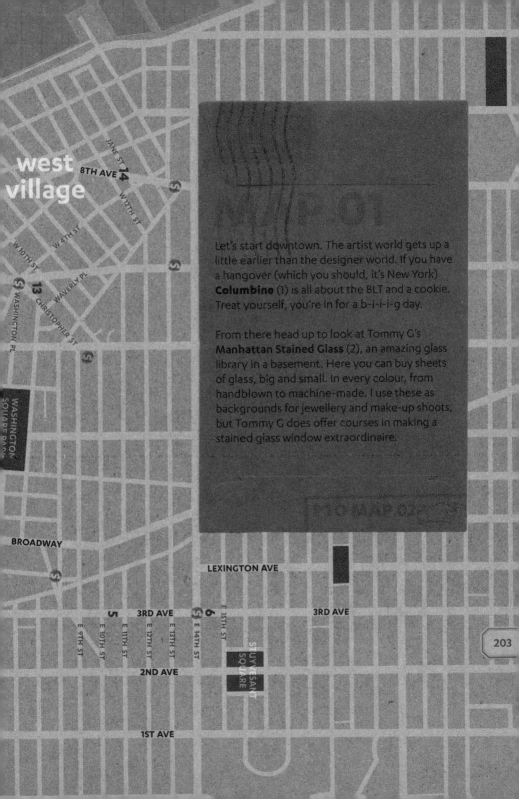

west village

8TH AVE **14**

JANE ST

W 12TH ST

W 4TH ST

W 10TH ST

WAVERLY PL

WASHINGTON PL

13 CHRISTOPHER ST

WASHINGTON SQUARE PARK

BROADWAY

LEXINGTON AVE

5 3RD AVE

6 3RD AVE

E 9TH ST

E 10TH ST

E 11TH ST

E 12TH ST

E 13TH ST

E 14TH ST

E 15TH ST

2ND AVE

1ST AVE

STUYVESANT SQUARE

Let's start downtown. The artist world gets up a little earlier than the designer world. If you have a hangover (which you should, it's New York) **Columbine** (1) is all about the BLT and a cookie. Treat yourself, you're in for a b-i-i-i-g day.

From there head up to look at Tommy G's **Manhattan Stained Glass** (2), an amazing glass library in a basement. Here you can buy sheets of glass, big and small. In every colour, from handblown to machine-made. I use these as backgrounds for jewellery and make-up shoots, but Tommy G does offer courses in making a stained glass window extraordinaire.

6TH AVE

BRYANT
PARK

W 42ND ST

W 43RD ST

5TH AVE

E 40TH ST

E 41ST ST

E 42ND ST

dear sibella –

it was a pleasure to finally

PURELY PAPER

For lovers of streamers, origami,
letters, cards, wrapping and
decorative paper, endpapers,
notebooks and journals,
confetti, envelopes, thank you
and personalised stationery,
stickers and stamps, this list
is for you!

* Confetti System
* Kate's Paperie
* New York Central Art Supply
* JAM Paper & Envelope
* Paper Presentation

Go up the road to **Pearl Paint** (3), a five storey mecca of all things art supply. There's a lift in the back corner — I always start at the top. Across Lispenard, they have a crafts and a paint specialty store as well.

Also on Canal Street is **Canal Plastics Center** (4), where they can pretty much make whatever your heart desires out of plexi in a short period of time. They have every shape under the sun (butterflies, skull and crossbones, unicorns, sailing ships, anything), ready to buy. I've been having things made here for shoots for many years and their coloured plastic selection is extensive.

Jump in a cab to another favourite store, **New York Central Art Supply** (5), and go straight to the second floor, to the paper department. Grab a scrap of paper and a small pencil from the desk to write down the codes from the paper samples. You will find these mounted, lining the walls. When you're done, give your notes to the quirky people behind the desk and off they go into paperland to find your supplies.

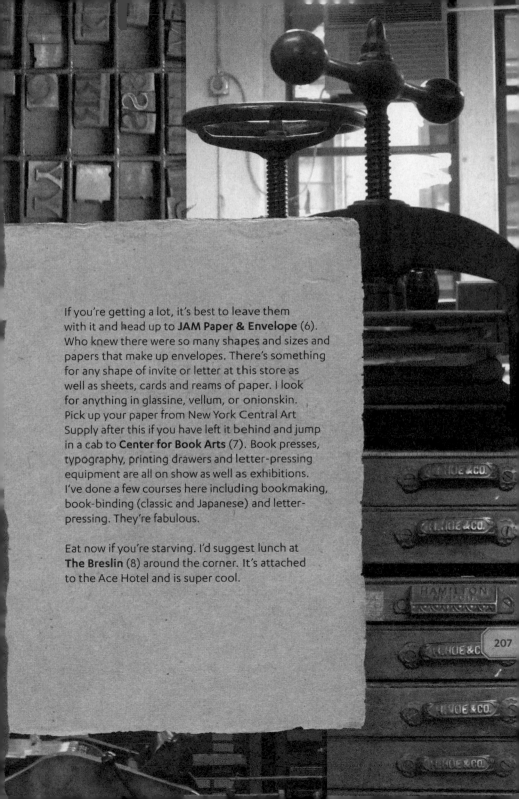

If you're getting a lot, it's best to leave them with it and head up to **JAM Paper & Envelope** (6). Who knew there were so many shapes and sizes and papers that make up envelopes. There's something for any shape of invite or letter at this store as well as sheets, cards and reams of paper. I look for anything in glassine, vellum, or onionskin. Pick up your paper from New York Central Art Supply after this if you have left it behind and jump in a cab to **Center for Book Arts** (7). Book presses, typography, printing drawers and letter-pressing equipment are all on show as well as exhibitions. I've done a few courses here including bookmaking, book-binding (classic and Japanese) and letter-pressing. They're fabulous.

Eat now if you're starving. I'd suggest lunch at **The Breslin** (8) around the corner. It's attached to the Ace Hotel and is super cool.

EVERY EXIT IS AN
ENTRANCE SOMEWHERE ELSE

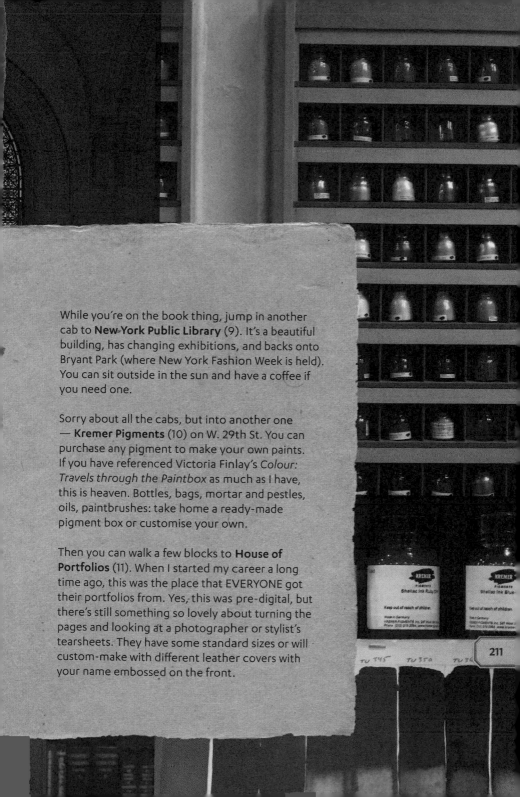

While you're on the book thing, jump in another cab to **New York Public Library** (9). It's a beautiful building, has changing exhibitions, and backs onto Bryant Park (where New York Fashion Week is held). You can sit outside in the sun and have a coffee if you need one.

Sorry about all the cabs, but into another one — **Kremer Pigments** (10) on W. 29th St. You can purchase any pigment to make your own paints. If you have referenced Victoria Finlay's *Colour: Travels through the Paintbox* as much as I have, this is heaven. Bottles, bags, mortar and pestles, oils, paintbrushes: take home a ready-made pigment box or customise your own.

Then you can walk a few blocks to **House of Portfolios** (11). When I started my career a long time ago, this was the place that EVERYONE got their portfolios from. Yes, this was pre-digital, but there's still something so lovely about turning the pages and looking at a photographer or stylist's tearsheets. They have some standard sizes or will custom-make with different leather covers with your name embossed on the front.

From there, walk to **The Set Shop** (12), which has everything you need for photo shoots, building sets and other industry stuff. What's not to love about a shop that supplies such a specific market. Containers of clear wedges, plexi cubes, clear wax, bull clips — you get the picture!

Jump on the train (A,C,E) on 8th Ave and 30th downtown to West 4th St and walk over to **Greenwich Letterpress** (13) on Christopher St. An old-fashioned, double-fronted store full of cards and all things paper. So much cooler than your average stationery store. Beth, the owner, can organise and design your letterpress cards and invites. It's usually a three-week wait and they can be shipped. If you really need them while you're in New York, you can order online and pick up when you get there.

And then walk south on 8th Ave to **The Ink Pad** (14) for all things that stamp. Every colour of stamping ink, stickers, rubber stamps and tags — this place makes scrap-booking look cool.

The next stop is **Compleat Sculptor** (15), about a 10 minute walk away.

Compleat Sculptor

Other than having every single sculpting and carving tool under the sun, they have an unexpected selection of raw wood and stone. Head past the moulding clays and wax at the rear of the shop and on the left, head through the clear plastic butchers' curtains to the basement. Be ready to be surprised. It's like walking into a small quarry. I love this space. The staff are very knowledgeable and there is an amazing note board at the front with courses, artists, suppliers etc.

90 Vandam St
NYC 10013
212.243.6074
www.sculpt.com

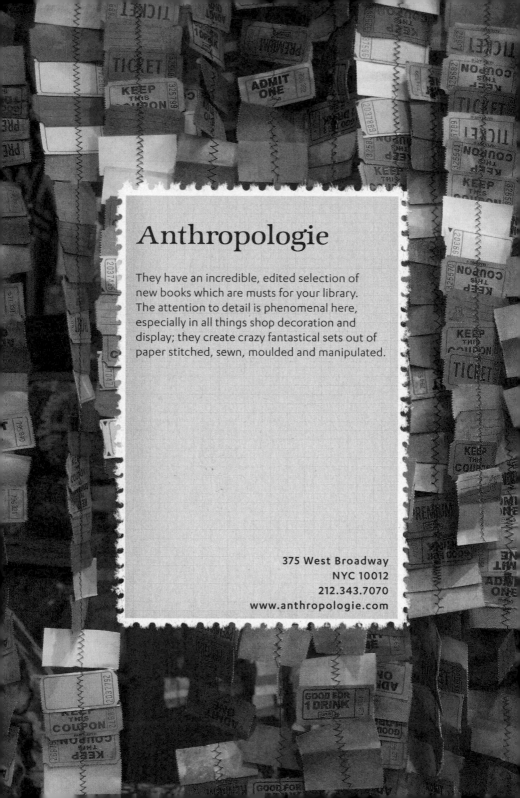

Anthropologie

They have an incredible, edited selection of
new books which are musts for your library.
The attention to detail is phenomenal here,
especially in all things shop decoration and
display; they create crazy fantastical sets out of
paper stitched, sewn, moulded and manipulated.

375 West Broadway
NYC 10012
212.343.7070
www.anthropologie.com

219

From **Anthropologie** (16), go to **Kate Spade** (17). Colourful Kate is not everyone's cup of tea but I go for the vintage book selection scattered throughout the store. I like it when big brands feel individual and handpicked. The stationery can be fun too, reminiscent of politer times!

Next is **Muji** (18). Plastic sleeves, the vellum post-it notes, the brown stitched notepads, mini rulers, the make-your-own weekly planner and the playing cards and the perfect pens. You cannot have too many.

Kate's Paperie (19) is a fantastic stationery shop that sells single sheet wrapping paper, cards, invites, craft supplies, rubber stamps, pens and coloured pencils, push-pins and has a customised invite/card service. I never tire of this place.

McNally Jackson (20). I love a boutique bookstore. So rare in New York nowadays. Support them as they have a great edited selection of great books, local information and cards plus a café!

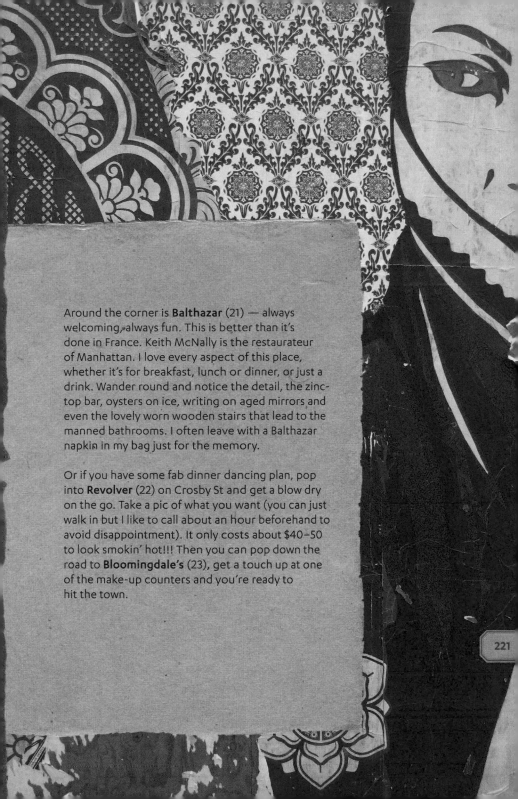

Around the corner is **Balthazar** (21) — always welcoming, always fun. This is better than it's done in France. Keith McNally is the restaurateur of Manhattan. I love every aspect of this place, whether it's for breakfast, lunch or dinner, or just a drink. Wander round and notice the detail, the zinc-top bar, oysters on ice, writing on aged mirrors and even the lovely worn wooden stairs that lead to the manned bathrooms. I often leave with a Balthazar napkin in my bag just for the memory.

Or if you have some fab dinner dancing plan, pop into **Revolver** (22) on Crosby St and get a blow dry on the go. Take a pic of what you want (you can just walk in but I like to call about an hour beforehand to avoid disappointment). It only costs about $40–50 to look smokin' hot!!! Then you can pop down the road to **Bloomingdale's** (23), get a touch up at one of the make-up counters and you're ready to hit the town.

paraph

1. Chelsea Antiques Garage / André's Tavern / 112 W. 25th St
2. New York Cake and Baking Distributor / 56 W. 22nd St
3. Cupcake Café / 18 W. 18th St
4. City Bakery / 3 W. 18th St
5. Fishs Eddy / 889 Broadway
6. Sara / 950 Lexington Ave
7. Dylan's Candy Bar / 1011 3rd Ave
8. Steuben / 667 Madison Ave
9. Calvin Klein / 654 Madison Ave
10. Tiffany & Co / 5th Ave and 57th St
11. Café Sabarsky / Neue Galerie / 1048 5th Ave
12. Bonnie Slotnick Cookbooks / 163 W. 10th
13. Global Table / 109 Sullivan St
14. Blue Ribbon Sushi / 119 Sullivan St
15. Broadway Panhandler / 65 E. 8th St
16. Astor Wines & Spirits / 399 Lafayette St
17. SOS Chefs / 104 Ave B
18. Russ & Daughters / 179 E. Houston St
19. Supper / 156 E. 2nd St

kitchen & table
ernalia

223

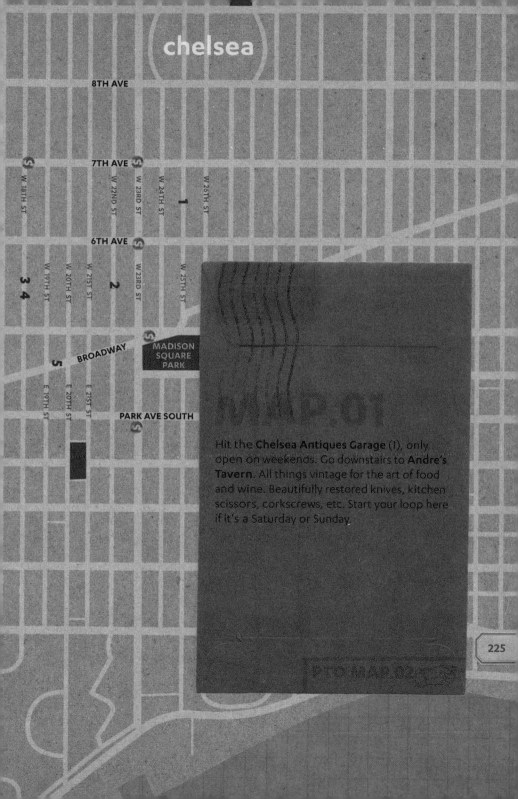

chelsea

8TH AVE

7TH AVE

W 18TH ST
W 22ND ST
W 23RD ST
W 24TH ST
W 26TH ST

1

6TH AVE

W 19TH ST
W 20TH ST
W 21ST ST
W 23RD ST
W 25TH ST

3 4
2

BROADWAY

5

E 19TH ST
E 20TH ST
E 21ST ST

MADISON
SQUARE
PARK

PARK AVE SOUTH

MAP.01

Hit the **Chelsea Antiques Garage** (1), only open on weekends. Go downstairs to **Andre's Tavern**. All things vintage for the art of food and wine. Beautifully restored knives, kitchen scissors, corkscrews, etc. Start your loop here if it's a Saturday or Sunday.

225

TO MAP.02

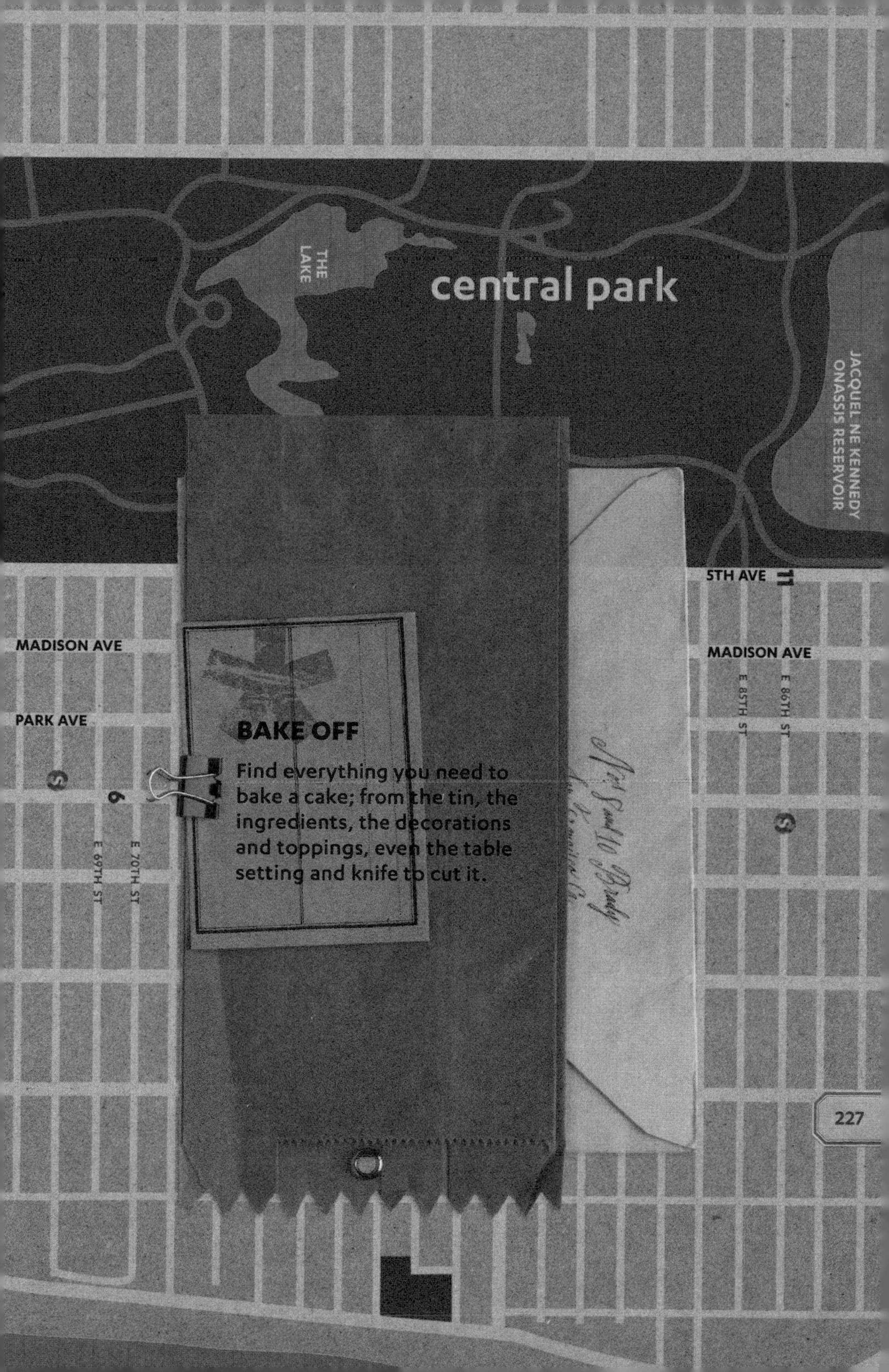

central park
THE LAKE
JACQUELINE KENNEDY ONASSIS RESERVOIR
5TH AVE
MADISON AVE
PARK AVE
MADISON AVE
E 85TH ST
E 86TH ST
E 69TH ST
E 70TH ST

BAKE OFF

Find everything you need to bake a cake; from the tin, the ingredients, the decorations and toppings, even the table setting and knife to cut it.

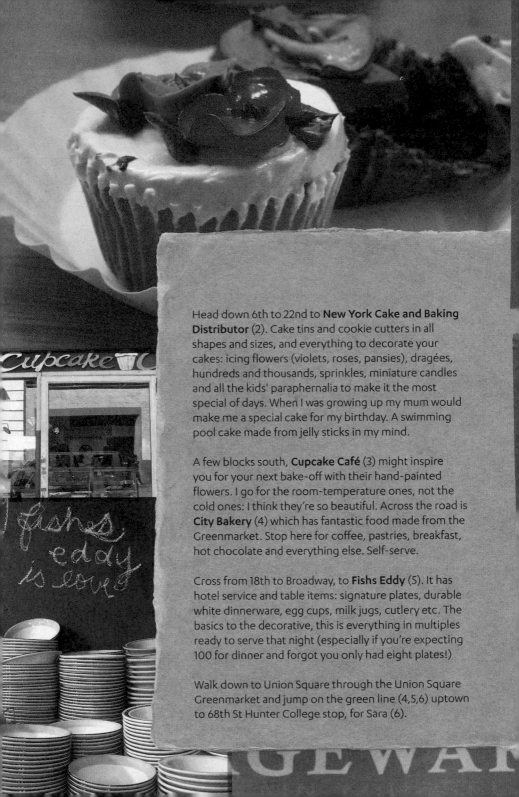

Head down 6th to 22nd to **New York Cake and Baking Distributor** (2). Cake tins and cookie cutters in all shapes and sizes, and everything to decorate your cakes: icing flowers (violets, roses, pansies), dragées, hundreds and thousands, sprinkles, miniature candles and all the kids' paraphernalia to make it the most special of days. When I was growing up my mum would make me a special cake for my birthday. A swimming pool cake made from jelly sticks in my mind.

A few blocks south, **Cupcake Café** (3) might inspire you for your next bake-off with their hand-painted flowers. I go for the room-temperature ones, not the cold ones: I think they're so beautiful. Across the road is **City Bakery** (4) which has fantastic food made from the Greenmarket. Stop here for coffee, pastries, breakfast, hot chocolate and everything else. Self-serve.

Cross from 18th to Broadway, to **Fishs Eddy** (5). It has hotel service and table items: signature plates, durable white dinnerware, egg cups, milk jugs, cutlery etc. The basics to the decorative, this is everything in multiples ready to serve that night (especially if you're expecting 100 for dinner and forgot you only had eight plates!)

Walk down to Union Square through the Union Square Greenmarket and jump on the green line (4,5,6) uptown to 68th St Hunter College stop, for Sara (6).

Sara

I have so many pieces from here. I go for the simpler plain bowls, cups in creams and browns but they also have some amazing organic platters. The owner showcases some great Japanese ceramicists and there is an ever-changing inventory. Take your time as it sometimes takes a minute to see the pieces individually. Once you understand, you will never want to drink out of a plain old manufactured handled mug ever again. And wait to watch the wrapping process (I have a piece I have never unwrapped).

950 Lexington Ave
NYC 10021
212.772.3243
www.saranyc.com

Walk downtown to **Dylan's Candy Bar** (7), set up by Ralph Lauren's daughter. In this Willy Wonka's factory, the floors are impregnated with floating candy. They specialise not only in American candy, but sweets from all over the world. It's packed to the rafters and smells like sugar from a few blocks away. Downstairs you can buy M&Ms in every colour by the bag.

Then west to **Steuben** (8), and go straight to the Ted Muehling tortoise range. I have coveted this for as long as the Georg Jensen gold bracelet watch! Icebucket and eight double old-fashioneds please.

From there, head to the minimalist mecca of **Calvin Klein**'s basement (9). Concrete floors, seamless shelves and Calvin Klein's tabletop range, bed linen and bathroom products. Expensive and beautiful, perfect to accompany loft living (if you have one).

Oh for a *Breakfast at Tiffany's* experience —
I don't know about you, but I love this movie. And I think of it every time I walk into **Tiffany & Co** (10). Ground floor is madness, so I go straight to the upper floors.

Catch the hidden lift secretly placed directly to your left as you walk in from the 5th Ave entrance. It's quicker and uncrowded.

I like looking at all the cutlery, especially the set that's stamped with Tiffany & Co. The playing cards are a personal favourite and come as a double pack, in classic Tiffany blue, in the stationery section. The frivolity of twig toothpicks and silver straws makes me smile and I must admit, I think I've bought a few in my time. The keyring for my shop is a silver shackle that I have had for over 15 years.

If you're hungry, there's a place that's a little off the loop. But very beautiful. Jump in a cab to the Neue Museum (housed in an old mansion) and sit in **Café Sabarsky** (11) and feel like you're in Vienna. You can have wine with your meal. Make sure you leave room for the amazing desserts!

Cab back to midtown.

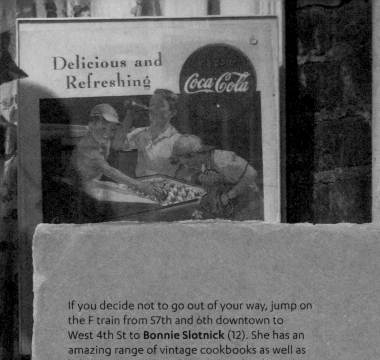

If you decide not to go out of your way, jump on the F train from 57th and 6th downtown to West 4th St to **Bonnie Slotnick** (12). She has an amazing range of vintage cookbooks as well as housekeeping manuals, etiquette books and culinary ephemera. I once asked Bonnie to find me a copy of the Australian book *Oh For a French Wife*, and she did. Cluttered not just with books but old wire utensils and all things packaged and tinned. Best to make an appointment.

Back on the subway at West 4th St on the downtown blue line (A,C,E) to Spring St. Walk east into SoHo to **Global Table** (13). I have so many tabletop items from here (I mean soooooooo many!) Plates, bowls, glasses, cups, vases, dishes, trays, mini-spoons, you name it, they have it. Something for every table shape and need, and very reasonably priced.

Have lunch at **Blue Ribbon Sushi** (14). I came here on my first trip to NYC when I was 22. And never stopped. It's a classic Japanese inn design, down to the red-leafed maple tree. Sit at the counter or in the booths. The wait can be long but it's open until two in the morning. I can't go past the eel and cucumber (wrapped on the outside) and the green tea crème brûlée. Experiment with the sake list — I choose by description and love drinking out of an overflowing sake box.

235

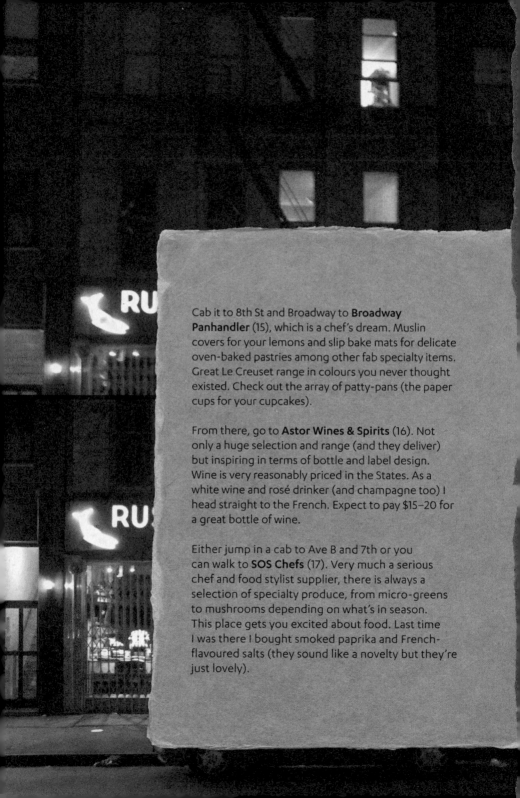

Cab it to 8th St and Broadway to **Broadway Panhandler** (15), which is a chef's dream. Muslin covers for your lemons and slip bake mats for delicate oven-baked pastries among other fab specialty items. Great Le Creuset range in colours you never thought existed. Check out the array of patty-pans (the paper cups for your cupcakes).

From there, go to **Astor Wines & Spirits** (16). Not only a huge selection and range (and they deliver) but inspiring in terms of bottle and label design. Wine is very reasonably priced in the States. As a white wine and rosé drinker (and champagne too) I head straight to the French. Expect to pay $15–20 for a great bottle of wine.

Either jump in a cab to Ave B and 7th or you can walk to **SOS Chefs** (17). Very much a serious chef and food stylist supplier, there is always a selection of specialty produce, from micro-greens to mushrooms depending on what's in season. This place gets you excited about food. Last time I was there I bought smoked paprika and French-flavoured salts (they sound like a novelty but they're just lovely).

Cruise down to Houston to the Jewish specialty food shop **Russ & Daughters** (18). I love this store — it smells good. I buy apricots and chocolate slabs with peanuts in it. But there's smoked fish and much more serious food than just snacks.

Time for some serious comfort food and good wine. I like sitting at the communal table at the front of **Supper** (19), or outside depending on the weather. Oh my god, everything's good on the menu. The meals are big so try and share. One of my favourites is the spaghetti with lemon. If a table isn't available straightaway, they have a wine bar next door that's always fun to wait in.

fu
&
in

niture
teriors

hudson river

tribeca

soho

CHRISTOPHER ST

HUDSON ST

7TH AVE

GREENWICH ST

HUDSON ST

N MOORE ST

VARICK ST

6TH AVE

BROOME ST

SPRING ST

WEST HOUSTON ST

8 9 10

W BROADWAY

W BROADWAY

WOOSTER ST

BLEECKER ST

E 3RD ST

11

WHITE ST

12

FRANKLIN ST

CHURCH ST

GRAND ST

GREENE ST

PRINCE ST

16

BOND ST

13

14

WALKER ST

CANAL ST

15

MERCER ST

17

DUANE ST

READE ST

BROADWAY

BROADWAY

18

19

CROSBY ST

LAFAYETTE ST

MULBERRY ST

MOTT ST

BOWERY

nolita

EAST HOUSTON ST

SARA D ROOSEVELT PARK

STANTON ST

1ST AVE

BROOME ST

DELANCEY ST

ORCHARD ST

21 22

23

LUDLOW ST

20

ESSEX ST

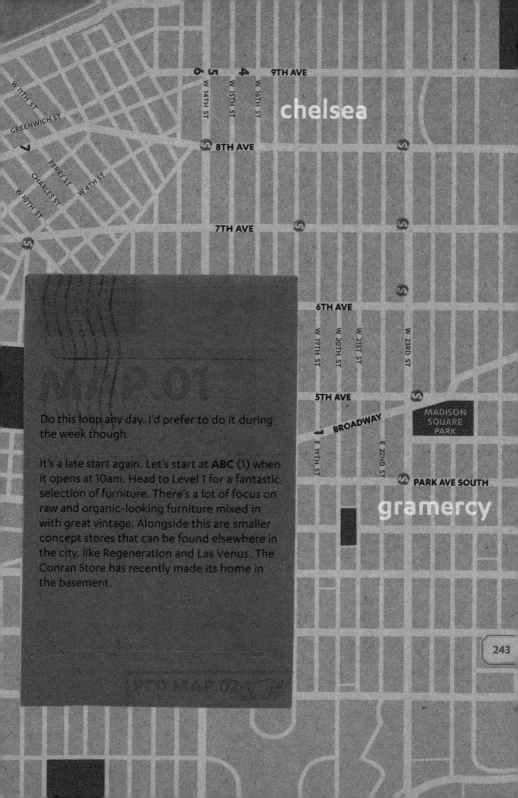

W 11TH ST

GREENWICH ST

PERRY ST

CHARLES ST

W 4TH ST

W 10TH ST

7

9TH AVE

6
5
4

W 14TH ST

W 15TH ST

W 16TH ST

chelsea

8TH AVE

7TH AVE

6TH AVE

W 19TH ST

W 20TH ST

W 21ST ST

W 23RD ST

5TH AVE

BROADWAY

1

E 19TH ST

E 22ND ST

MADISON
SQUARE
PARK

PARK AVE SOUTH

gramercy

Do this loop any day. I'd prefer to do it during the week though.

It's a late start again. Let's start at **ABC** (1) when it opens at 10am. Head to Level 1 for a fantastic selection of furniture. There's a lot of focus on raw and organic-looking furniture mixed in with great vintage. Alongside this are smaller concept stores that can be found elsewhere in the city, like Regeneration and Las Venus. The Conran Store has recently made its home in the basement.

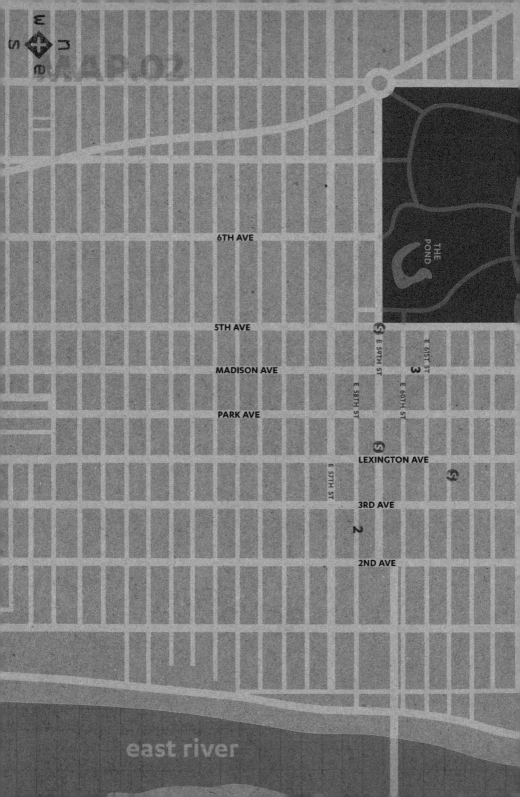

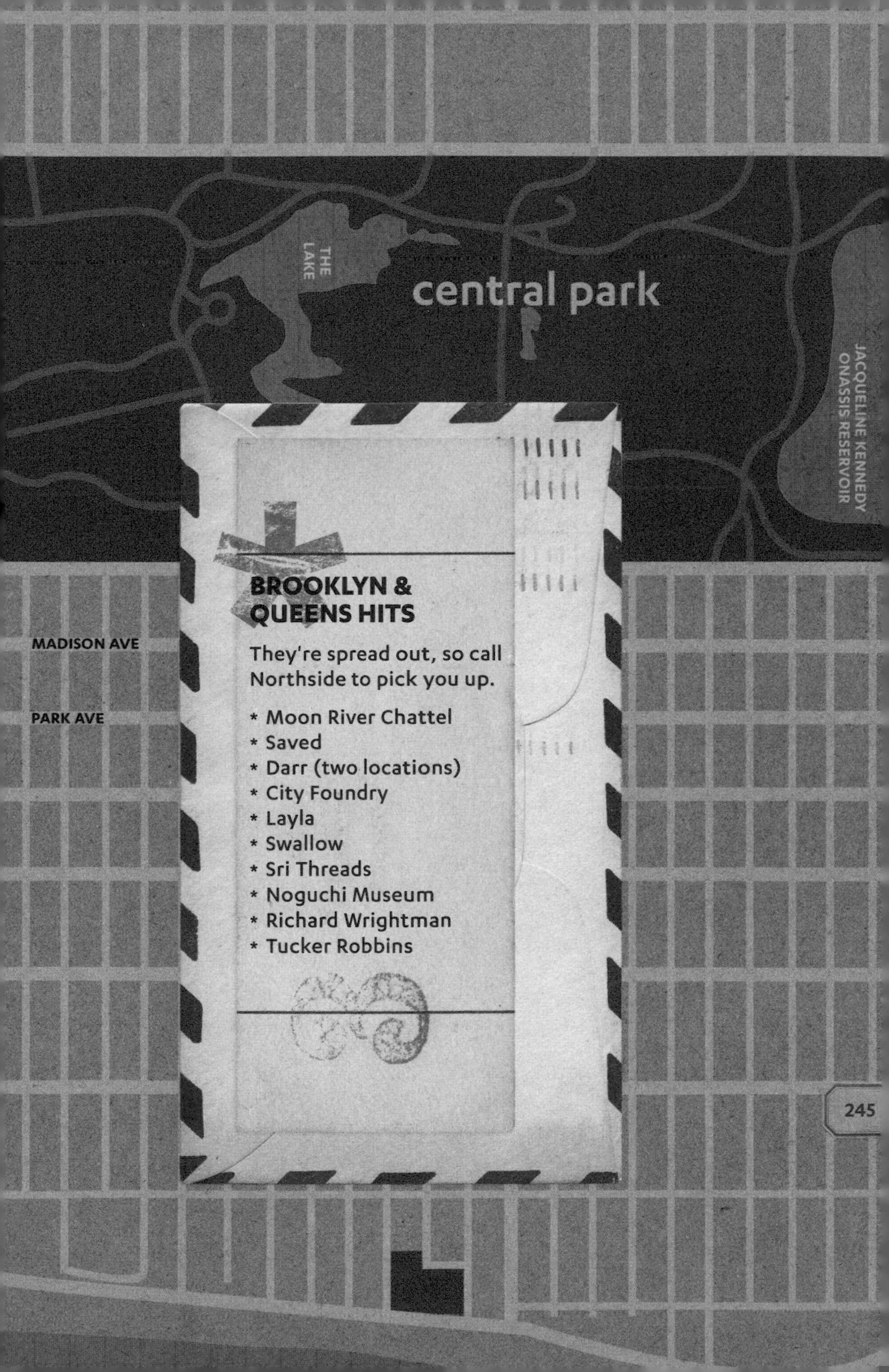
THE LAKE
central park
JACQUELINE KENNEDY ONASSIS RESERVOIR
MADISON AVE
PARK AVE

BROOKLYN & QUEENS HITS

They're spread out, so call Northside to pick you up.

* Moon River Chattel
* Saved
* Darr (two locations)
* City Foundry
* Layla
* Swallow
* Sri Threads
* Noguchi Museum
* Richard Wrightman
* Tucker Robbins

At Union Square, jump on the subway and take the yellow (N,R) uptown to 5th Ave for **Interieurs** (2). They used to be located a block from my house in Tribeca and I rented their split bamboo black tables hundreds of times. A mix of industrial furniture pieces sit with this Asian-French style. Great accessories — my favourite vase, of hand-blown glass into chicken wire, comes from here.

Next is **Chelsea Passage** (3) on the 9th floor of Barneys. It showcases an array of fancy (and not always expensive) homewares, furniture and tableware. It covers all price points and still has a sense of humour, thanks to Barneys creative director Simon Doonan.

Cab it downtown to 15th and 9th Ave and grab a coffee at **Ninth Street Espresso** (4) in the Chelsea Market.

Check out the glass floating staircase at the **Apple Store** (5). I could look at this for hours. Fantastic engineering.

I'm not a fan of **Hugo Boss** (6) clothes, but this is a spectacular interior. The history of the space (an old meatpacking warehouse) has been maintained and a skeleton framework, reminiscent of the inside of Moby Dick, built by Italian architect Matteo Thun.

Walk over to the sea of colour that is **The End of History** (7). Mostly Scandinavian and Italian mid-century glass and ceramics. Every shape and size imaginable interspersed with furniture. From the organic to the minimal. The collection is very specific and obsessively edited by the owner.

Walk down to the cluster of antique shops on 6th Ave between Houston and Prince. I've never known the names of these but have bought many things, from handblown glass to framed molluscs. On sunny days, their wares spill onto the street. Jump on a train at Houston St downtown to Chambers St. There are quite a few shops on Duane St, mostly antique.

Working Class's (8) owner David dreamt of coming to New York in his youth, and never looked back. Part shop, part boutique ad agency (downstairs), he stocks all things British: Paul Smith, silver vintage tea sets and perfume bottles sourced in the UK. He has his own line of T-shirts, bags, perfumes, candles. Look hard — there are treasures.

Mondo Cane (9) is one of the serious antique/interior stores. Recently they were exhibiting and selling their Carl Auböck collection. Carefully selected mid-century/modern furniture and accessories.

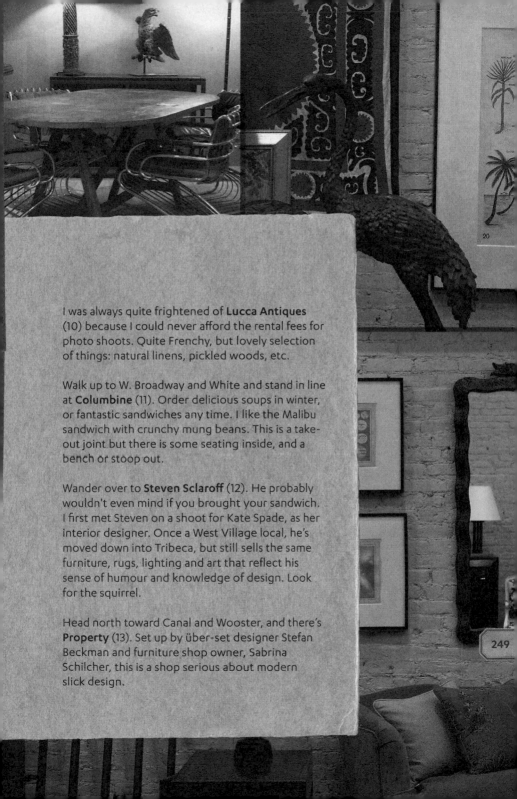

I was always quite frightened of **Lucca Antiques** (10) because I could never afford the rental fees for photo shoots. Quite Frenchy, but lovely selection of things: natural linens, pickled woods, etc.

Walk up to W. Broadway and White and stand in line at **Columbine** (11). Order delicious soups in winter, or fantastic sandwiches any time. I like the Malibu sandwich with crunchy mung beans. This is a take-out joint but there is some seating inside, and a bench or stoop out.

Wander over to **Steven Sclaroff** (12). He probably wouldn't even mind if you brought your sandwich. I first met Steven on a shoot for Kate Spade, as her interior designer. Once a West Village local, he's moved down into Tribeca, but still sells the same furniture, rugs, lighting and art that reflect his sense of humour and knowledge of design. Look for the squirrel.

Head north toward Canal and Wooster, and there's **Property** (13). Set up by über-set designer Stefan Beckman and furniture shop owner, Sabrina Schilcher, this is a shop serious about modern slick design.

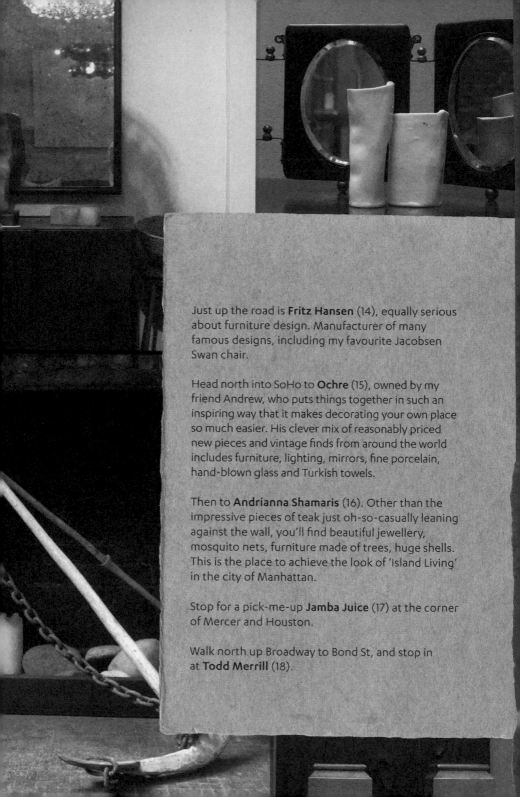

Just up the road is **Fritz Hansen** (14), equally serious about furniture design. Manufacturer of many famous designs, including my favourite Jacobsen Swan chair.

Head north into SoHo to **Ochre** (15), owned by my friend Andrew, who puts things together in such an inspiring way that it makes decorating your own place so much easier. His clever mix of reasonably priced new pieces and vintage finds from around the world includes furniture, lighting, mirrors, fine porcelain, hand-blown glass and Turkish towels.

Then to **Andrianna Shamaris** (16). Other than the impressive pieces of teak just oh-so-casually leaning against the wall, you'll find beautiful jewellery, mosquito nets, furniture made of trees, huge shells. This is the place to achieve the look of 'Island Living' in the city of Manhattan.

Stop for a pick-me-up **Jamba Juice** (17) at the corner of Mercer and Houston.

Walk north up Broadway to Bond St, and stop in at **Todd Merrill** (18).

Todd Merrill

This antique furniture store is a taste of Hollywood in Manhattan. Seriously glamorous: mirrored dressers, Murano glass chandeliers, gold-leafed objets and other fab pieces to deck out your super-fancy, super-fabulous loft!

65 Bleecker St
NYC 10012
212.673.0531
www.merrillantiques.com

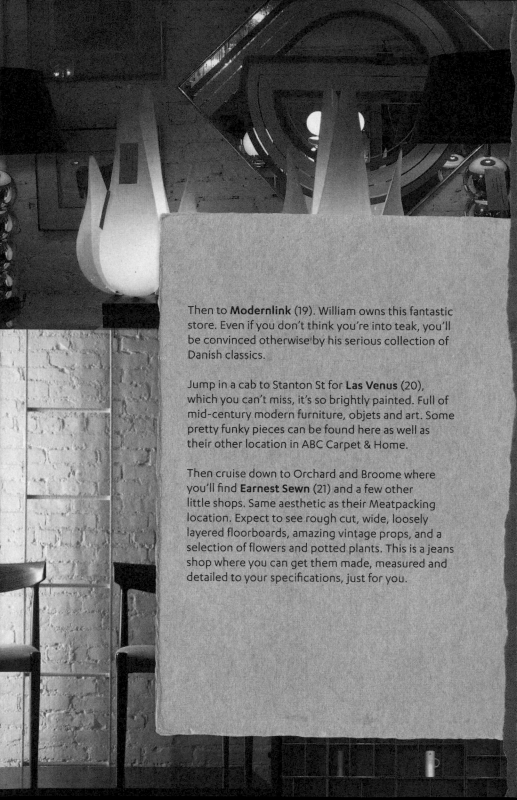

Then to **Modernlink** (19). William owns this fantastic store. Even if you don't think you're into teak, you'll be convinced otherwise by his serious collection of Danish classics.

Jump in a cab to Stanton St for **Las Venus** (20), which you can't miss, it's so brightly painted. Full of mid-century modern furniture, objets and art. Some pretty funky pieces can be found here as well as their other location in ABC Carpet & Home.

Then cruise down to Orchard and Broome where you'll find **Earnest Sewn** (21) and a few other little shops. Same aesthetic as their Meatpacking location. Expect to see rough cut, wide, loosely layered floorboards, amazing vintage props, and a selection of flowers and potted plants. This is a jeans shop where you can get them made, measured and detailed to your specifications, just for you.

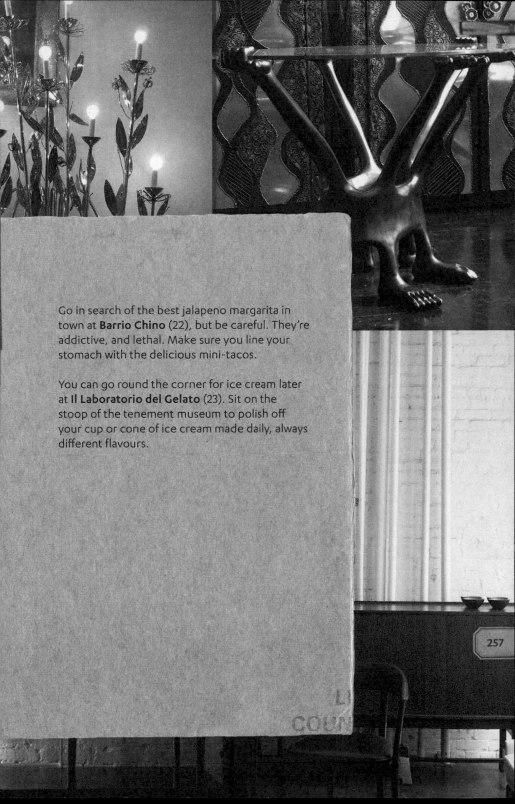

Go in search of the best jalapeno margarita in town at **Barrio Chino** (22), but be careful. They're addictive, and lethal. Make sure you line your stomach with the delicious mini-tacos.

You can go round the corner for ice cream later at **Il Laboratorio del Gelato** (23). Sit on the stoop of the tenement museum to polish off your cup or cone of ice cream made daily, always different flavours.

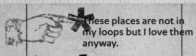

These places are not in my loops but I love them anyway.

index

a

261

e

Earnest Sewn   143, 256
821 Washington St
NYC 10006
212.242.3414
90 Orchard St
NYC 10002
212.979.5120
www.earnestsewn.com

Electric Trading Co   *
313 Canal St
NYC 10013
212.226.0575
For anything to do with lighting – cloth
covered cords, Bakelite fittings and
aluminium shades.

Elizabeth Street Gallery   37
209 Elizabeth St
NYC 10012
212.941.4800
www.elizabethstreetgallery.com

The End of History   247
548 ½ Hudson St
NYC 10014
212.647.7598
http://theendofhistory.blogspot.com

E. R. Butler & Co.   112
(by appt)
55 Prince St
NYC 10012
212.925.3565
www.erbutler.com

Erica Tanov   *
204 Elizabeth St
NYC 10012
212.334.8020
www.ericatanov.com
People constantly ask me where I get my
fine gold jewellery – well, this is one of
the places.

Erie Basin   *
388 Van Brunt St Brooklyn
NYC 11231
718.554.6147
www.eriebasin.com

E. Vogel   106
19 Howard St
NYC 10013
212.925.2460
www.vogelboots.com

Evolution   69
120 Spring St
NYC 10012
212.343.1114
www.theevolutionstore.com

f

Fishs Eddy   228
889 Broadway at 19th St
NYC 10003
877.347.4733
www.fishseddy.com

45 rpm   34
169 Mercer St
NYC 10012
917.237.0045
www.rby45rpm.com

Fred's   42
Barneys
9th floor
660 Madison Ave
NYC 10065
212.833.2200

Freemans   80, 121
End of Freemans Alley, Off Rivington
between the Bowery and Chrystie.
NYC 10002
212.420.0012
www.freemansrestaurant.com

Freemans Sporting Club   *
8 Rivington St
NYC 10002
212.673.3209
www.freemanssportingclub.com
This is a shop for MEN. Lumberjack kinda
men. It's got a barber out the back, and it's
just cool to be seen in here.

Fritz Hansen   252
22 Wooster St
NYC 10013
212.219.3226
www.fritzhansen.com

The Future Perfect   194
55 Great Jones St
NYC 10012
212.473.2500
www.thefutureperfect.com

263

g

George Taylor Specialties Inc 105
76 Franklin St
10013
212.226.5369

Gimme! Coffee *
228 Mott St
NYC 10012
212.226.4011
www.gimmecoffee.com
Serves fantastic coffee. Check out the
locks on the fence next door. I've heard it
means 'locks of love'.

Global Table 234
109 Sullivan St
NYC 10012
212.431.5839
www.globaltable.com

G. Page 24
120 W. 28th St
NYC 10001
212.741.8928
www.gpage.com

Gramercy Park Hotel *
2 Lexington Ave
NYC 10010
212.920.3300
www.gramercyparkhotel.com
I stayed here for months at a time before
it was renovated, but now it's all fancy.
Have a drink and check out the foyer by
Julian Schnabel with the butterfly-wing
art and the custom-made Moooi charred
pool table.

Grandaisy Bakery 65
73 Sullivan St
NYC 10012
212.334.9435
www.grandaisybakery.com

Greenwich Letterpress 212
39 Christopher St
NYC 10014
212.989.7464
www.greenwichletterpress.com

Guggenheim Museum 180
1071 5th Ave
NYC 10128
212.423.3500
www.guggenheim.org

h

Habu 141
135 W. 29th St #804
NYC 10001
212.239.3546
www.habutextiles.com

Haus Interior 194
250 Elizabeth St
NYC 10012
212.741.0455
www.hausinterior.com

Hester St Fair *
Hester and Essex St
NYC 10002
Small flea market on the Lower East
Side. Vintage clothes, tools, some new
jewellery and delicious macaroons. (Sat &
Sun 10–6, April–December)

The High Line 46
529 W. 20th St #8W
NYC 10011
212.206.9922
www.thehighline.org

House of Portfolios 211
48 W. 21st St 6th fl.
NYC 10010
212.206.7323
www.houseofportfolios.com

Hugo Boss 246
401 W. 14th St
NYC 10011
646.336.8170

Hyman Hendler & Sons 132
21 W. 38th St
NYC 10018
212.840.8393
www.hymanhendler.com

i

IF 146
94 Grand St
NYC 10013
212.334.4964

265

k

Shuts at 4 and I just love that this place still exists in this area, a specialty store that literally just supplies soles, shoelaces and the like to bootmakers.
....

A great room and a good stop for lunch in Soho. Canteen-style, Asian (Thai-ish) food that is sometimes difficult to find in New York city.
....

Before they became globally available; I loved going to this original outpost. Now a double shop, there's lots to choose from in their ever-expanding hair and beauty range. Buy something and you can get as many samples as you like.
....

l

m

McNally Jackson 220
52 Prince St
NYC 10012
212.274.1160
www.mcnallyjackson.com

Madeline Weinrib Atelier 155
ABC Carpet & Home
888 Broadway 6th floor
NYC 10003
212.473.3000
www.madelineweinrib.com

Makié 143
109 Thompson St
NYC 10012
212.625.3930
www.makieclothier.com

Manex USA 142
126 W. 25th St
NYC 10001
800.699.6466
www.manex-usa.com

Manhattan Laminates *
624 W. 52nd St
NYC 10019
212.255.2522
www.manhattanlaminates.com
Huge range of finishes – I mean hundreds
of different surfaces. You buy in standard
4' x 8' sheets. Great for backgrounds for
shooting on as well as a building material.
You can purchase sample chips so they are
ready at hand

Manhattan Stained Glass 203
79 Leonard St
NYC 10013
646.613.1420.
www.manhattanstainedglass.com.

**Manhattan Wardrobe
Supply** 135
245 W. 29th St 8th floor
NYC 10001
212.268.9993
www.wardrobesupplies.com

Mantiques Modern 64
146 W. 22nd St
NYC 10011
212.206.1494
www.mantiquesmodern.com

Marlow & Sons *
81 Broadway
Williamsburg
NYC 11211
718.384.1441
www.marlowandsons.com

Matta 146
241 Lafayette St
NYC 10012
212.343.9399
www.mattany.com

Matter 194
405 Broome St
NYC 10012
212.343.2600
www.mattermatters.com

Mecox Gardens 43
962 Lexington Ave
NYC 10021
212.249.5301
www.mecoxgardens.com

The Mercer 171
147 Mercer Street
NYC 10012
212.966.6060
www.mercerhotel.com

The Met 43
1000 5th Ave at 82nd St
NYC 10028
212.535.7710
www.metmuseum.org

Metalliferous 91
34 W. 46th St
NYC 10036
212.944.0909
www.metalliferous.com

Michele Varian 77
35 Crosby St
NYC 10013
212.226.1076
www.michelevarian.com

Milk Studios *
450 W. 15th St
NYC 10011
212.645.2797
www.milkstudios.com
If you need a studio to photograph the
hottest, latest, greatest piece of furniture
or person, this is the place for you. This
is what they call a super studio. You are

guaranteed to run into famous people in the foyer or café or in the übercool digital studio bar. If you need more, they have a gallery that can exhibit you, a production company and a penthouse and roof terrace available for shoots or party hire.

M & J Trimming 132
1008 6th Ave
NYC 10018
212.204.9595 or1800 9MJ TRIM
www.mjtrim.com

Modernlink 256
35 Bond St
NYC 10012
212.254.1300
www.modernlink.com

Mogador *
101 St. Marks Place
NYC 10009
212.677.2226
www.cafemogador.com
Best Moroccan in town (not that I can think of anywhere else). Great on a winter's night for Casablanca chicken tagine or breakfast in any season. I have Middle-Eastern eggs which I still crave: scrambled eggs with hummus, tabouli and harissa with flat bread.

MoMa 186
11 W. 53rd St
NYC 10019
212.708.9700
www.moma.org

Mondo Cane 247
174 Duane St
NYC 10013
212.219.9244
www.mondocane.come

Moon River Chattel *
62 Grand St Brooklyn
NYC 11211
718.388.1121
www.moonriverchattel.com

Moss 193
150 Greene St
NYC 10012
212.204.7100
www.mossonline.com

Mudtruck 153
307 E. 9th St
NYC 10003
often at Broadway and 14th NYC 10002 or Astor Place NYC 10003
212.529.8766
www.themudtruck.com

Muji 135, 220
455 Broadway
NYC 10013
212.334.2002
620 8th Ave
NYC 10018
212.382.2300
www.muji.us

n

New York Cake and Baking Distributor 228
56 W 22nd St
NYC 10010
212.675.2253 (212.675.CAKE)
www.nycake.com

New York Central Art Supply 206
62 3rd Ave
NYC 10003
212.473.7705
www.nycentralart.com

New York Elegant Fabrics 134
222 W. 40th St
NYC 10018
212.302.4980
www.nyelegantfabrics.com

New York Public Library 211
5th Ave and 42nd St
NYC 10018
www.nypl.org

Nicole Farhi *
75 9th Ave
NYC 10011
646.638.1173
www.nicolefarhi.com
Soft furnishings range include linen napkins, lambswool throws and other tactile, desirable, expensive pieces.

Ninth Street Espresso 246
75 9th Ave
NYC 10011
212.228.2930
www.ninthstreetespresso.com

269

Pearl River 70
477 Broadway
NYC 10013
212.431.4770
www.pearlriver.com

P. E. Guerin (by appt) *
23 Jane St
NYC 10014
212.243.5270
www.peguerin.com
It's hard to believe they cast their own
metal on site, especially in the heart of
the West Village. A great catalogue, and
many things can be shipped or bought
immediately. They also custom make.

Planter Resource 24
New York City Flower Market
150 W. 28th St
NYC 10001
212.206.7687 (212.206.POTS)
www.planterresource.com

The Plaza 180
5th Ave, Central Park South
NYC 10019
212.759.3000
www.theplaza.com
The Plaza recently became residential –
but the Palm Court is still intact and worth
a look-in if you need to use the bathroom.

Prince Lumber *
404 W. 15th St, corner of 9th Ave and
15th St
NYC 10014
212.777.1150
www.princelumber.com
If you need any wood cut and delivered
in the city for any building project, these
guys are great. There are not many lumber
suppliers in the city and they have a full
hardware store too.

Printed Matter, Inc. 187
195 10th Ave
NYC 10011
212.925.0325
www.printedmatter.org

Property 249
14 Wooster St
NYC 10013
917.237.0123
www.propertyfurniture.com

Purl 146
459 Broome St
NYC 10012
212.420.8796
www.purlsoho.com

r

Regeneration *
38 Renwick St
NYC 10013
212.741.2102
www.regenerationfurniture.com
Two levels of mid-century furniture. A
cool little street – Giorgio DeLuca (of
Dean & DeLuca) lives on it.

Remains *
130 W. 28th St
NYC 10001
212.675.8051
www.remains.com
Right in the heart of the flower market,
this lighting shop sells fabulous vintage
pieces and has its own line of vintage-
inspired lighting.

Revolver 221
590 Broadway
NYC 10012
212.219.9626
www.revolversalon.com

Richard Wrightman (by appt) *
44-01 11th St
Long Island City
NYC 11101
718.707.0217
www.richardwrightman.com

Ricky's 34
590 Broadway
NYC 10013
212.226.5552
www.rickysnyc.com

RRL 112
31 Prince St
212.343.0841
NYC 10012
390 Bleecker St
212.462.4390
NYC 10014
www.ralphlauren.com

R 20th Century *
82 Franklin St
NYC 10013
212.343.7979
www.r20thcentury.com
A serious store dedicated to mid-century
design. One day I might be able to
afford one of their beautiful lights.

The Rug Company 171
88 Wooster St
NYC 10012
212.274.0444
www.therugcompany.info

Russ & Daughters 239
179 East Houston St
NYC 10002
212.475.4880
www.russanddaughters.com

S

Santa Maria Novella 37
(in Lafco New York)
285 Lafayette St
NYC 10012
212.925.0001
www.lafcony.com

Sara 231
950 Lexington Ave
NYC 10021
212.772.3243
www.saranyc.com

Saved *
426 Union Ave Williamsburg Brooklyn
NYC 11211
718.486.0850
www.savedtattoo.com

Schiller's Liquor Bar *
131 Rivington St
NYC 10002
212.260.4555
www.schillersny.com
Go to the bathroom: it's communal and
has great tapware. I like coming here in
the summer for the vodka lemonade and
all the little interior details. Keith McNally
in true spirit. Check out the wine list and
painted bottles numbered from no.1
CHEAP no.2 DECENT no.3 GOOD.

Schoolhouse Electric 100
27 Vestry St
NYC 10013
212.226.6113
www.schoolhouseelectric.com

Secondhand Rose 158
230 5th Ave #510
NYC 10010
212.393.9002
www.secondhandrose.com

The Set Shop 212
36 W. 20th St
NYC 10011
212.255.3500
www.setshop.com

Shake Shack 158
Madison Square Park, near Madison Ave
and E. 23rd St
NYC 10010
212.889.6600
www.shakeshack.com

Shapiro Hardware *
63 Bleecker St
NYC 10012
212.477.4180
Hand-cut tacks, cable ties, shower curtain
hooks and all the things you don't see
anywhere else in the world.

Smith & Mills 99
71 N. Moore St
NYC 10013
212.226.2515
www.smithandmills.com

Snack 65
105 Thompson St
NYC 10012
212.925.1040

SOS Chefs Inc 238
104 Ave B
NYC 10009
212.505.5813
www.sos-chefs.com

Sri Threads (by appt) *
18 Eckford St #8 Brooklyn
NYC 11222
718.599.2559
www.srithreads.com
Stephen has an amazing selection of
mainly Japanese textiles, particularly
indigo things. This is a secret I really
struggled with giving up, but you gotta
support your friends.

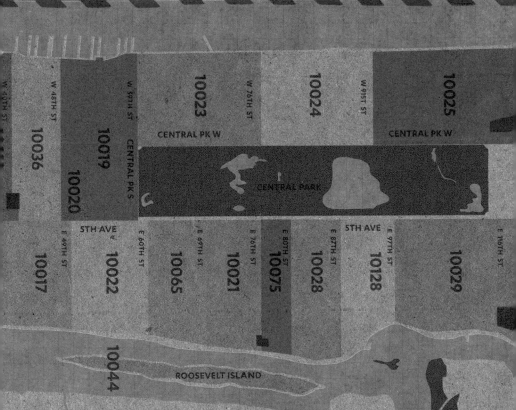

W 40TH ST

W 48TH ST

10036

W 59TH ST

10019

CENTRAL PK W

10020

10023

W 76TH ST

CENTRAL PK W

10024

W 91ST ST

10025

CENTRAL PK W

CENTRAL PK S

CENTRAL PARK

5TH AVE

E 49TH ST

5TH AVE

E 60TH ST

E 69TH ST

E 76TH ST

E 80TH ST

E 87TH ST

E 97TH ST

5TH AVE

E 106TH ST

10017

10022

10065

10021

10075

10028

10128

10029

10044

ROOSEVELT ISLAND

zipcodes

zipcode index

10001

10002

10029

Central Park 261
Conservatory Garden
5th Ave and 105th St
Central Park
Garden

10036

Joe
44 Grand Central Terminal
Coffee

Metalliferous 91
34 W. 46th St
Jewellery supplies

10038

Dim Sum Go Go 262
5 E. Broadway (on
Chatham Square)
Dumplings and yum cha

10065

Barneys 42
660 Madison Ave
Homewares

Calvin Klein 232
654 Madison Ave
Homewares

Chelsea Passage 246
Barneys
660 Madison Ave
Homewares

Fred's 42
Barneys
9th floor
660 Madison Ave
Food

Steuben 232
667 Madison Ave
Glassware

10075

Lady M 267
41 E. 78th St
Cakes

Wolford 146
997 Madison Ave
Stockings

10128

Cooper-Hewitt 180
2 E. 91st St (and corner
of 5th Ave)
Museum

Guggenheim Museum 180
1071 5th Ave
Museum

BROOKLYN & QUEENS

Brook Farm General 260
Store
75 Sth. 6th St Brooklyn
NYC 11211
Hardware and garden

City Foundry 261
365 Atlantic Ave Brooklyn
NYC 11217
*Industrial furniture
and lighting*

Darr 262
369 Atlantic Ave Brooklyn
NYC 11217
*Vintage furniture and
accessories*

Diner 262
85 Broadway Brooklyn
NYC 11211
Food and drink

Erie Basin 263
388 Van Brunt St Brooklyn
NYC 11231
Jewellery and the unusual

Layla 267
86 Hoyt St Brooklyn
NYC 11201
Textiles and jewellery

Moon River Chattel 269
62 Grand St Brooklyn
NY 11211
*Vintage furniture,
housewares, garden
and bath*

Marlow & Sons 268
81 Broadway Brooklyn
NY 11211
Food and wine

Noguchi Museum 270
9-01 33rd Rd (at Vernon
Boulevard)
Long Island City
NY 11106
Museum

Richard Wrightman 271
(by appt)
44-01 11th St Long Island
City
NYC 11101
Campaign furniture

Sri Threads 272
(by appt)
18 Eckford St #8 Brooklyn
NYC 11222
Japanese textiles

Swallow 273
361 Smith St Brooklyn
NYC 11231
Glassware and accessories

Saved 272
426 Union Ave
Williamsburg Brooklyn
NYC 11211
Tattoo parlour

Tucker Robbins 274
33-02 Skillman Ave 4th fl.
Long Island City
NYC 11101
Furniture

Published in 2011
by Murdoch Books Pty Limited

Murdoch Books Australia
Pier 8/9, 23 Hickson Road
Millers Point NSW 2000
Phone: +61 (0) 2 8220 2000
Fax: +61 (0) 2 8220 2558
www.murdochbooks.com.au

Murdoch Books UK Limited
Erico House, 6th Floor
93–99 Upper Richmond Road
Putney, London SW15 2TG
Phone: +44 (0) 20 8785 5995
Fax: +44 (0) 20 8785 5985
www.murdochbooks.co.uk

Publisher: Diana Hill
Concept and design: Reuben Crossman
Editor: Leta Keens
Production: Alexandra Gonzalez

National Library of Australia Cataloguing-in-Publication Data
Author: Court, Sibella
Title: The Stylist's Guide to NYC / Sibella Court
ISBN: 978-1-74266-108-7 (hbk.)
Subjects: Art--New York (State)--New York--Guidebooks. Design--New York (State)--
New York--Guidebooks. New York (N.Y.)--Description and travel--Guidebooks.
Dewey Number: 700.97471

A catalogue record for this book is available from the British Library.

Printed by 1010 Printing International Limited, China.

THANK YOU

Edwina McCann, Erez Schernlicht, Katie Dineen, James Merrell, Jonny Valiant,
Amber Jacobsen, Jee, Randy & Sebastian, Leah Rauch, Chris Court, my dad,
Peter and my family, Donna Hay, Hannah Brady, Reuben Crossman, Kay Scarlett,
Katrina O'Brien, Diana Hill, Leta Keens and all the shopowners of NYC:
Thank you for letting me stay at your apartment, lending me your bike, editing
& organising, taking pictures, going to the library, allowing me into your space,
loving beautiful things, enduring retail in really hard times, driving me around,
having lunch & drinks in supercool restaurants & bars, getting up early for
markets & fact checking!!